Searching for a Self

Identity in Popular Culture, Media and Society

by

Arthur Asa Berger
San Francisco State University

Series in Sociology
VERNON PRESS

www.vernonpress.com

In the Americas:
Vernon Press
1000 N West Street, Suite 1200,
Wilmington, Delaware 19801
United States

In the rest of the world:
Vernon Press
C/Sancti Espiritu 17,
Malaga, 29006
Spain

Series in Sociology

Library of Congress Control Number: 2021947354

ISBN: 978-1-64889-487-9

Also available: 978-1-64889-328-5 [Hardback]; 978-1-64889-390-2 [PDF, E-Book]

Illustrated with drawings and photographs by the author.

Cover design by Vernon Press using drawings created by the author.

To my grandchildren, Ariel, Kavanna, Seth, and Noah

Table of Contents

The events of people's lives have, after all, only to the least degree originated in them, having generally depended on all sorts of circumstances such as the moods, the life or death of quite different people, and have, as it were, only at the given point of time come hurrying towards them. For in youth life still lies before them as an inexhaustible morning, spread out all around them full of everything and nothing; and yet when noon comes there is all at once something there that may justly claim to be their life now, which is, all in all, just as surprising as if one lay suddenly there were a man sitting there before one, with whom one had been corresponding for twenty years without knowing him, and all the time imagining him quite different. But what is still much queerer is that most people do not notice his at all; they adopt the man who has come to stay with them, whose life has merged with their own lives and whose experiences now seem to them the expression of their own qualities, his destiny their own merit or misfortune. Something has had its way with them like a fly-paper with a fly; it has caught them fast, here catching a little hair, there hampering their movements, and has gradually enveloped them, until they lie buried under a thick coating that has only the remotest resemblance to their original shape....

Robert Musil, *The Man Without Qualities*

List of Illustrations

List of Tables

Acknowledgments

I would like to thank all the philosophers, scholars, journalists and writers, of all kinds, who have supplied me with material on the subject of identity that helped shaped my thinking about the subject and whose writings I have quoted throughout the book. I use quotations so my readers can see what the writers and theorists from whom I quote had to say and how they expressed themselves. I also am grateful to my wife Phyllis for proofreading the manuscript, truly a labor of love, and to the editors and production staff of the Vernon publishers.

Thanks, also, to the people who have contributed short boxed inserts on subjects of their expertise:

Nina Savelle-Rocklin,
A psychoanalyst and author located in Los Angeles.

Chris Arning,
A semiotician, and president of Creative Semiotics in London.

Christian Fuchs,
A Marxist scholar, and professor at Westminster University in London.

Dirk vom Lehn,
A sociologist, and professor at King's College in London.

Preface:
Takeaways from *Searching For a Self*

After reading this book you will have learned something about:

1. The basic concepts of semiotic theory of Ferdinand de Saussure and Charles S. Peirce, and how the study of signs can help us understand identity better. Among the topics discussed are biosemiotics, hairstyles, eyeglass styles, facial expressions, and body language.
2. Important concepts from sociological theorists such as Emile Durkheim and Pierre Bourdieu and how they can be applied to the study of identity. This chapter will deal, among other things, with informal high school groups, national character, and individualism.
3. Some ideas of Freud and other psychoanalysts such as Erik Erikson, which help us understand the psyche and identity. The discussion will also deal with identification authenticity and borderline personalities.
4. Theorists such as Karl Marx, Vladimir Lenin, Fritz Pappenheim, and Erich Fromm about alienation and other topics that can be applied to the study of identity.
5. The existence of a remarkable book by Nigel Dennis, *Cards of Identity,* that is about a club that can change people's identities to suit the club's purposes by discovering their most "useful" identities.
6. The important and destructive role that Vodka plays in Russian culture and other aspects of Russian identity involving a theory about how some Russian babies were raised and its cultural impact.
7. The "Impostor Syndrome," discussed in my academic mystery *Mistake in Identity,* and how it can be applied to Donald Trump to explain his psyche and behavior.
8. "The Broadway Riders," who wear the clothes of motorcycle riders but don't have motorcycles, as a case study of the role of fashion in identity.
9. Contemporary theories about gender, with a focus on the ideas of Judith Butler about gender as a "performance" and how these ideas can be applied to "non-binary" Lesbian, Gay, Bisexual, Transsexual, Queer, Intersexual, and Asexual people.
10. The way the clothes of Orthodox Jewish people help establish their religious identities and set them off from non-Orthodox Jews and non-Jews.

11. The ideas of the Marxist semiotician Roland Barthes, as found in his book *Mythologies,* about various mystifying aspects of contemporary French culture.
12. The role that tattoos play in shaping people's identities.
13. The "cult" cars made by Porsche and the role of these cars in the lives of people who own this brand of automobile and enjoy the benefits of "German engineering."
14. How elite universities perform branding for their students and the role this branding plays in their lives.
15. The role membership in the Republican Party plays in shaping people's political identities, plus a fanciful theory about how the toilet training of children is related to their membership in the Republican Party. The enigma of the 2020 election and the role that working-class authoritarianism plays in the Republican Party are also considered.
16. How taking cruises is connected to the myth of Odysseus and how cruising creates an identity for people that they find positive. The discussion also deals with different typologies for travelers and the notion that tourists are now "models" for modern mankind.

Part I:
Theories of Identity

Chapter 1
Introduction

> Gentlemen, this is an historic moment for the Identity Club....Our beloved theory, the only true one in the world, is the only one we want to hear about. Identity is the answer to everything. There is nothing that cannot be seen in terms of identity. We are not going to pretend that there is the slightest argument about *that.* We of this club excel all other clubs in that we give our patients the identities they can use best. We can make all sorts of identities, from Freudian to Teddy Boy to Marxist and Christian. We are the idea behind the idea, the theory at the root of theory. And what we like about ourselves is the frank work we go about our work. Other clubs stubbornly deny that they try to supply their patients with new identities. They insist that they merely reveal an identity that has been pushed out of sight. Thank God, gentlemen we shall never be like them! We are proud to know that we are in the very van of modern development that we can transform any unknown quantity into a fixed self, and that we never fall back on the hypocrisy or pretending we are mere uncoverers.
>
> Nigel Dennis, *Cards of Identity*

How do people turn out the way they do? How they "arrive" at themselves and attain an identity. There are countless matters to consider when dealing with identity, which, as Nigel Denis reminds us, "is the answer to everything." How are our identities affected by our birth order, by our hair color, by how tall or short we are, by our intelligence, by our occupation, by our race, by our religion, by our nationality, by the socio-economic level of our parents (or our being raised in a single-parent family), by where we are born and where we grow up, by the language we learn, by the way we use language, by our fashion tastes, by our gender, by our education, by our psychological makeup, by chance experiences we have, by the people we marry (if we marry) and by countless other factors.

Robert Musil on The Man Without Qualities

In Robert Musil's great novel, *The Man Without Qualities,* he offers some insights into what happens to people as they progress through what we call now the life cycle. He begins with a chilling simile: that at some moment in our lives we suddenly become strangers to ourselves and it is as if we were flies that had been slowly covered over with the kind of glue found on flypaper and don't recognize how this happened.

Figure 1.1: Robert Musil.

Drawing by the author.

When we were young, he adds, our lives are full of urgency and intensity, only to give way, in our middle years, to our becoming someone we cannot recognize. He writes (1965:152):

> When we are young we have a force of resistance in us and that our scorn for the established order and revolt against it are nothing but "fluttering" attempts to fly and nothing we do is caused by an inner necessity even if everything we dash at seems incredibly necessary and urgent.

The urgency of our youth has been tamed and, as the result of all kinds of things we do, of chance events, of mistakes we make or good choices we make, we end up like flies on flypaper, more or less stuck with the identity that has, in some mysterious manner, taken over our lives.

How Our Lives Escape From Us

Let me offer an example of how our lives can "escape" from us. Many years ago, on an airporter bus from the Los Angeles airport to the University of Southern California, for an interview about teaching there for a year, the bus driver said, to one of the passengers, "This isn't the life I expected to lead. I'm a saxophone player, not a bus driver." Many people probably have the same feeling about their lives. They find, in midlife, that they aren't living the lives they expected to live. When they were young, they had certain expectations but for one reason or another, things didn't work out the way they thought they would. As the years pass, they experience some kind of subtle acquiescence and end up living lives quite different from what they imagined they would and their sense of possibility is never realized.

Chapter 2
The Semiotics of Identity

> Everything we do sends messages about us in a variety of codes, semiologists contend. We are also on the receiving end of innumerable messages encoded in music, gestures, foods, rituals, books, movies, or advertisements. Yet we seldom realize that we have received such messages and would have trouble explaining the rules under which they operate.
>
> Maya Pines, "How They Know What You Really Mean."
> *San Francisco Chronicle.* Oct. 13, 1982.

> The basic unit of semiotics is the *sign* defined conceptually as something that stands for something else, and, more technically, as a spoken or written word, a drawn figure, or a material object unified in the mind with a particular cultural concept. The sign is this unity of word-object, known as a *signifier* with a corresponding, culturally prescribed content or meaning, known as a *signified.* Thus our minds attach the word "dog," or the drawn figure of a "dog," as a signifier to the idea of a "dog," that is, a domesticated canine species possessing certain behavioral characteristics. If we came from a culture that did not possess dogs in daily life, however unlikely, we would not know what the signifier "dog" means. . . . When dealing with objects that are signifiers of certain concepts, cultural meanings, or ideologies of belief, we can consider them not only as "signs," but *sign vehicles.*
>
> Mark Gottdiener, *The Theming of America: Dreams, Visions, and Commercial Spaces.*

What we learn from Maya Pines, quoted in the epigraph, is that we are always sending messages about ourselves and, at the same time, receiving messages sent by others. And it is the task of semiotics, the science of signs, to understand how messages work and how to interpret these messages correctly. We all are amateur semioticians when we indulge in people-watching, but we seldom think as precisely and as granularly as semioticians when it comes to analyzing these messages—technically known in semiotics as signs.

Semiotics: The Science of Signs

The science of semiotics, as we know it now, is based on the work of two scholars: a Swiss linguistics professor, Ferdinand de Saussure, and an American philosopher who taught at Harvard University, Charles Sanders Peirce.

Figure 2.1: Ferdinand de Saussure.

Drawing by the author.

It is useful to quote from Saussure's book, *Course in General Linguistics,* to see what he said about signs (1915/1966: 16):

> Language is a system of signs that expresses ideas, and is therefore comparable to a system of writing, the alphabet of deaf-mutes, symbolic rites, polite formulas, military signals, etc. But it is the most important of these systems. A science that studies the life of signs within society is conceivable; it would be part of social psychology and consequently of general psychology; I shall call it *semiology* (from Greek *sēmeîon* "sign."). Semiology would show what constitutes a sign, what laws govern them.

Saussure wrote that signs have two parts: a sound-image or *signifier* and a concept or meaning, what he called the *signified* generated by the signifier. It is important to know that the relation between the *signifier* and *signified* is not natural or permanent but is arbitrary and based on convention. Thus, the meaning of signs can change over time. He showed the relationship between signifiers and signified in the diagram shown below.

Figure 2.2: Signifier/Signified Relationship.

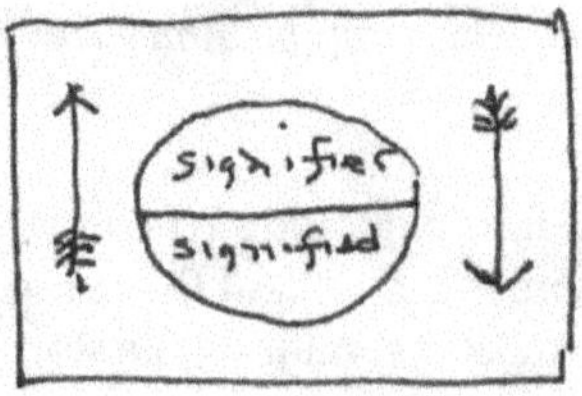

Berger after Saussure

Saussure offered a major insight into the concepts or meanings generated by signifiers. Concepts, he explained, are always defined differentially. We always think about concepts in terms of polar oppositions. Thus, no sign has meaning by itself; its meaning is always a function of its relationship with other signs.

C.S. Peirce offers another insight into the semiotics of identity:

> It seems a strange thing, when one comes to ponder over it, that a sign should leave its interpreter to supply part of its meaning; but the explanation of the phenomenon lies in the fact that the entire universe—not merely the universe of existents, but all that wider universe, embracing the universe of existents, as a part, the universe which we are all accustomed to refer to as "the truth"—that all this universe is perfused with signs, if it not composed exclusively of signs.
>
> https://richardcoyne.com/2018/03/10/pansemiotics/

Semiotics, we see, is an imperialist science, which is interested in everything in a universe perfused with signs. When we are dealing with concepts, because of the nature of language, we tend to think in terms of polar oppositions such as cheap and expensive, rich and poor, happy and sad. We learn to interpret signs as we grow up and learn, informally, the codes that tell us what signs mean. Daniel Chandler, a semiotician, explains the relationship between signs and codes in his book *Semiotics: The Basics* (2002:147):

> Since the meaning of a sign depends on the code within which it is situated, codes provide a framework within which signs make sense. Indeed, we cannot grant something the status of a sign if it does not function within a code....The conventions of codes represent a social dimension in semiotics: a code is a set of practices familiar to users of the medium operating with a broad cultural framework....When studying cultural practices, semioticians treat as signs any objects or actions which have meaning to the members of a cultural group, seeking to identify the rules or conventions of the codes which underlie the production of meaning within that culture.

Pines explained that the signs we are talking about involve gestures, foods, rituals, and just about everything we say and do, what we look like, how we talk, and so on. This is because objects and other kinds of signs have meaning and semiotics helps us understand how to make sense of these signs. What follows is a discussion of biosemiotics and then an exercise in applied semiotics in which the science is applied to various aspects of people's identities.

Biosemiotics and the Self

Biosemiotics is an aspect of semiotics that expands our notion of what semiotics is from a focus on what we might call the "discrete self" to the relation between a self, as we commonly think about a self and semiotics, to other living forms, from cells in our bodies to societies. For example, some biologists now argue that the micro-organisms in our gut play an important role in our decision-making and other aspects of our lives. That is, we are, in certain respects, ruled by our stomachs.

Susan Petrelli, a professor of linguistics at the University of Bari, offers an overview of the subject in her article "Modelling, dialogue, and globality: Biosemiotics and Semiotics of self. 2. Biosemiotics, semiotics of self, and semiotic ethics" which appeared in *Sign System Studies,* 31.1.2005:

> The main approaches to semiotic inquiry today contradict the idea of the individual as a separate and self-sufficient entity. The body of an organism in the micro- and macrocosm is not an isolated biological entity, it does not belong to the individual, it is not a separate and self-sufficient system in itself. The body is an organism that lives in relation to other bodies.

Her focus, here, is in focusing our attention on the fact that we are part of nature and connected in important ways to all the other organisms and animals found in nature. We find an expanded version of this idea in the two quotations from biosemioticians that follow.

Timo Maran, a professor of semiotics at the University of Tartu in Finland, offers an insight into what biosemiotics has to say about the self and identity in his article on the "Semiotic self: perspectives for biosemiotics and cognitive semiotics." He writes:

> The concept of "semiotic self" appears to problematize the physicalist view of the subject, so human's semiotic activity, a unique description, a configuration of signs, and therefore in principle not fixed in although dependent on the physical "realness". By emphasizing the semiotic nature of processes, by which the subject is created, the "semiotic self" may provide a more semiotic and elaborate understanding of this topic. We can bring out the following principal properties of the concept of "semiotic self": 1. It is a result of semiotic processes. It arises from the modeling based on different codes available in the living organism. 2. It is rooted in biological semiotic processes. On the most primitive level it derives from the functioning of the immunological system and other processes, by which the organismal self is distinguished from its surrounding. 3. It is not a singular unit, but rather emerges from the compound or collective processes on different organizational levels (similarly to Hoffmeyer's (1997) swarming body). 4. It is a dynamical entity that allows the development of the self, misidentification of the self and even a virtual projection of the self, thus including also an environmental perspective. 5. It has a layered structure that joins both biological and cultural (linguistic, narrative) semiotic processes and enables these to be analyzed in the same conceptual framework. The

> concept appears to have potential for developing a broader description of a semiotic subject.
>
> https://www.sol.lu.se/doc/1294600084.conference.721.pdf.0.Maran_semiotic_self.pdf/Maran_semiotic_self.pdf

Biosemiotics, we see, adds a biological perspective to the semiotics of identity and semiotics of all kinds. There are now journals devoted to the subject and the field offers conferences attended by scholars in many disciplines. It turns out that human beings aren't the only organisms that are semiotic in nature and biosemiotics sees human beings as more connected to other animals and organisms than many people imagine.

Paul Cobley, another semiotician who teaches in England and has written extensively about biosemiotics, offers the following insights into biosemiotics and the self in his article, "The Cultural Implications of Biosemiotics" which was published May 21, 2010, online in the journal *Biosemiotics*:

> In conclusion, the first observation to make is that the most obvious cultural implication of biosemiotics is its abolition of the individual/collectivity dyad. The problematising of individualism which arises from the 'swarm' of humanity identified by biosemiotics is as striking as the realization that what drives the plot of Michael Crichton's 2006 novel, Prey, is the liquidity of humans and the illusory solidity of their boundaries. The self, considered as bounded by the skin, is a sham; it has to be reconsidered with reference to other, just as plausible, boundaries which might include family and community. Biosemiotics thus serves well those cultural analyses and philosophies that have been suspicious of individualism. The other obvious cultural implication of biosemiotics is its abolition of the grounds for dividing living nature and culture. All its findings and arguments, none more so than those made by Sebeok, demonstrate that logically, scientifically and culturally, culture should only be considered as existing within nature. Yet, in addition, biosemiotics makes an indispensable contribution to a future reorientation of the humanities. Many biosemiotics central figures are interested in non-human organisms; but, in reality, biosemiotics is carried out by humans and is about humans. What has largely been discussed in this article, in fact, is the problem of reflections on humans derived from studies predominantly concerned with life that is non-human.
>
> https://www.academia.edu/323835/The_Cultural_Implications_of_Biosemiotics

What we learn from Cobley is that the development of biosemiotics has led to a new sense of how the humanities can be understood and studied. Biosemiotics doesn't accept the binary split between nature and culture which has been foundational in most of the thinking about these two topics. If the biosemioticians are correct, the concept of the "self" *bounded by the skin* is, as Cobley puts it, "a sham," and an illusion since it sees people as disconnected in important ways to entities such as life that is non-human and as well as the family and community. He adds (personal communication):

> On the self, there is a great article by Sebeok from 1979, followed up by 3 others over the years. There, he posits the self as arising at the level of the cell, in association with the immune system's recognition of what is not the self. That is done partly with respect to the protectiveness of the cell's membrane, but also beyond, such that organisms develop their own "bubble".

Biosemiotics is, "suspicious" of individualism, which, it argues, incorrectly tends to separate the self from other members of the biosphere. This matter of identifying culture as within nature is a revolutionary concept. We can still talk about identity and the search for a self, though for biosemioticians, that search has to be seen as taking place within nature rather than culture.

Another scholar, Bill Sullivan, argues that hidden biological forces play an important role in our lives and shape much of our behavior. As he explains in his article, "Why You Like What You Like," (*National Geographic*, Vol.236, No. 3, 09/2009:17-18):

> There may be nothing more self-defining than our tastes. Whether in food, wine, romantic patterns, or political candidates, our tastes represent our identities. So it made sense to me that my likes and dislikes were formed through careful deliberation and rational decision-making—that is through choices where I wielded some control....As I dug into the scientific literature, I hit upon this astonishing and unsettling truth: Our actions are governed by hidden biological forces—which is to say that we have little or no control over our personal tastes. Our behaviors and preferences are profoundly influenced by our genetic makeup, by factors in the environment that affect our genes, and by other genes forced into our system by the innumerable microbes that dwell inside us....

There are, it seems, social and biological forces that shape our preferences in many areas of our lives. One aspect of our bodies that plays an important role in the way we present ourselves to others that is biological in nature, but social and cultural in the way we deal with it, is our hair, which is discussed next. It is genetics that gave us the kind of hair we have and helps us decide what to do with it.

Hair

When people look at other people, while people-watching, they notice many things, all more or less at the same time. We notice the color of people's hair and the way their hair is styled or displayed. Women have many different hairstyles, and over the course of their lives, often change them. And, in many cases, they change their hair colors.

Only two percent of people are born with blonde hair and in the United States, because we have so many Caucasians, that figures to five percent. This means that most of the people with blonde hair have dyed their hair. Only two percent of people have naturally red hair, so most of the redheads you see have dyed their hair, though dying one's hair red is not as popular as dying one's hair blonde.

Figure 2.3: Blonde Hair.

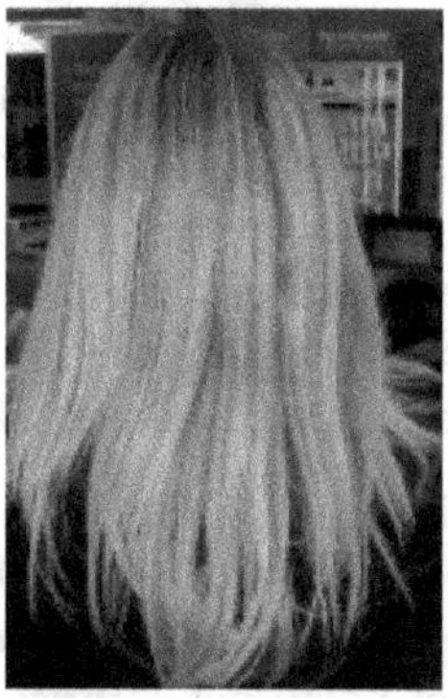

Photo by the author.

As a result of the obsession women have with their hair colors and hairstyles, the "beauty" parlor industry is an enormous one, all over the world. In recent years, men have become concerned with their hairstyles, and in barbershops, now, you have many choices you can make. The old choices, "short" or "long," have been replaced by very complicated hairstyles such as:

High Skin Fade + Hard Part Comb Over
Crew Cut + High Fade and Full Beard
Thick Curly Hair +High Bald Taper Fade
Textured Top + Taper Fade and Beard
Slick Back Undercut + Long Beard
Buzz Cut + Fade
High Skin Pompadour + Beard
Braided Razor Cut with Pompadour

Let's take a look at an example of creativity in men's hairstyles in the image below.

Figure 2.4: High Fade Loose Pompadour Hair Style.

Drawing by Author.

Roland Barthes, an important French semiotician, dealt with the way hair sends messages in an article on the way Romans are portrayed in films. In his book *Mythologies,* he discusses the way the director of a film communicated, to his audiences, that men were Romans. There is a chapter in the book "The Romans in Films" that explains that the most important signifier of Roman-ness in men is the frontal lock on their foreheads. He writes (1972:26, 27):

> Everyone is reassured, installed in the quiet certainty of a universe without duplicity, where Romans are Romans thanks to the most legible of signs: hair on the forehead.... In the category of capillary meanings, here is a subsign, that of nocturnal surprises. Portia and Calpurnia, woken up at the dead of night, have conspicuously uncombed hair.

Signs must be meaningful to people and so, for the audiences of the film *Julius Caesar,* it is the hairstylists who provide signs that the general public can easily and immediately understand. And that is because they have learned, by watching other films about Romans, that the most direct and easily recognized signifier of Roman-ness is "hair on the forehead" of males. In the film, the uncombed hair of Portia and Calpurnia are signifiers of "nocturnal surprises," and the inability of these women to comb their hair. I can only imagine what Barthes would have written about the English Prime Minister, Boris Johnson, whose hair is always unkempt. It functions as a signifier of Johnson just the way Trump's hair was probably the most important signifier of Trump.

I happen to be one of the two percent of Americans with naturally red hair and, when I was younger, of very bright red hair. My wife asked me, the other day, whether I'd be the same person had my hair been brown or black. An interesting question. Although I am now eighty-eight years old, my hair is still red, but not as bright as it was when I was a child. The photograph of me shown below was taken around ten years ago when I was seventy-eight years old. In the years since then, my hair has become lighter, but it is still red. It is difficult to dye hair red and have it come out looking good, which explains why many women have told me, over the years, "I'd kill for that color hair. It is a shame it was wasted on a man."

Figure 2.5: Photo of Arthur Asa Berger.

Photo by Phyllis Berger.

Some years ago, there was an article in the *San Francisco Chronicle* about what different hairstyles for men and women signified. The article, by the business editor, Donald White, on Dec. 20, 1980, "Office Life: Executives Can Lose by a Hair," dealt with hairstyles and the business world. His article was based on a poll of 200 hairstylists in the San Francisco Bay area about what they considered to be the least attractive hairstyles of business executives. Here is a chart I made, based on the findings of this poll, that offers commonly held opinions and attitudes about the messages conveyed by different hairstyles for men and women at the time.

Table 2.1: The Meaning of Hairstyles.

The Meaning of Male Hairstyles	
hair parted to hide baldness	phoniness, self-consciousness
shoulder length hair	anti-establishment values
greased hair	too slick, not trustworthy
curly permanent grown out	sloppy, disinterested
crew cut	old fashioned, inflexible
The Meaning of Female Hairstyles	
Punk Rock	anti-authority, belligerence
back-combed, bouffant	archaic, can't embrace new ideas
feathered in front, long in back	Teeny-Bopper, lack of maturity
severely streaked	cheapness, low morals

Table by the Author.

Now, women dye their hair in many different colors: purple, green, and orange, to convey messages about themselves. Hairstyles play an important role in many religions—both as a means of differentiating an individual with a given hairstyle from others and of identifying an individual with a particular religion or sect or some kind of a religious entity. Consider, here, the hairstyles of traditional Orthodox Jews, who distance themselves from non-Jews and non-Orthodox Jews with their long side locks (called "payot"). There are distinctive hairstyles in many other religions: think, here, of Franciscan monks and Buddhist priests. These hairstyles, we may say, are manifestations of self-discipline and the rules found in various religions.

Eyeglasses and Sunglasses

Many years ago, while my wife and I were waiting in an airport in Mexico for a flight to San Francisco, a woman came over to a kiosk to purchase a pair of sunglasses and spent at least thirty minutes trying on different styles of sunglasses and looking at herself in a mirror--trying to decide which one she liked best. Obviously, she recognized that her choice of a style and brand of sunglasses would convey something about her to anyone who looked at her. We can say the same thing about regular eyeglasses. They say something about our sense of style. Everything we say or don't say, when some kind of response is expected, or do or don't do when it is assumed we will do something, can be seen as a sign, and in terms of this discussion a message.

Figure 2.6: President Joe Biden with Aviator Sunglasses.

White House Photo.

There are many different styles of sunglasses and one's choice of a sunglass style functions as a message about the person's personality and sense of self. Many journalists have commented on President Joe Biden's Ray-Ban aviator sunglasses which he wears frequently and which the *Wall Street Journal* described as a "political statement."

Implicit in the aviator style of sunglasses or glasses is a connection with authority and adventure (pilots are seen as having high status and an exciting kind of life) and even modernity, even though the aviator design was created more than eighty years ago. In allaboutvision.com, we read:

> This classic glasses style, launched in 1936 to protect pilots' peepers, took off when Marlon Brando's biker donned them in 1951's "The Wild One," then soared as a perennial via Tom Cruise's flyboy in 1986's "Top Gun."
>
> https://www.allaboutvision.com/frames/men.htm

So there is also an element of celebrity connected to aviator-style sunglasses, and the fact that sunglasses, of all kinds, have an element of disguise to them. When you wear dark sunglasses, people cannot see whether you are looking at them which gives you an element of disguise and distancing that clear eyeglasses do not provide.

Facial Expressions

Our faces are our most prominent non-verbal means of providing information about us to others. Our faces are the most important means we have of displaying our emotions and can inform others of many things about us, such as our personalities, trustworthiness, and motivations. Paul Ekman, a psychologist and probably the most important scholar involved with facial research, has studied facial expression all over the world and suggests that eight facial expressions are universal (though many other facial expressions are not):

> Anger
> Determination
> Disgust
> Fear
> Neutral
> Pouting
> Sadness
> Surprise

In a report, "*Facial expression understanding*" that Ekman wrote for the National Science Foundation (with Terrence J. Sejnowski), we read:

> Faces are accessible "windows" into the mechanisms which govern our emotional and social lives. The technological means are now in hand to develop automated systems for monitoring facial expressions and animating artificial models. Face technology of the sort we describe, which is now feasible and achievable within a relatively short time frame,

could revolutionize fields as diverse as medicine, law, communications, and education.

Facial expressions provide information about:
affective state, including both emotions such as fear, anger, enjoyment, surprise, sadness, disgust, and more enduring moods such as euphoria, dysphoria, or irritableness;

cognitive activity, such as perplexity, concentration, or boredom; temperament and personality, including such traits as hostility, sociability, or shyness;

truthfulness, including the leakage of concealed emotions, and clues as to when the information provided in words about plans or actions is false;

psychopathology, including not only diagnostic information relevant to depression, mania, schizophrenia, and other less severe disorders, but also information relevant to monitoring response to treatment.

http:// face-and-emotion.com/database/nsfrept/exec_sumary.html.

Our facial expressions are an important means of establishing our identities and various aspect of our identities: our personalities, our character, and our emotional states. Semiotically speaking, our facial expressions can be seen as signifiers that can reveal a great deal about us.

Figure 2.7: Irfan Essa's images from Ph.D. Dissertation.

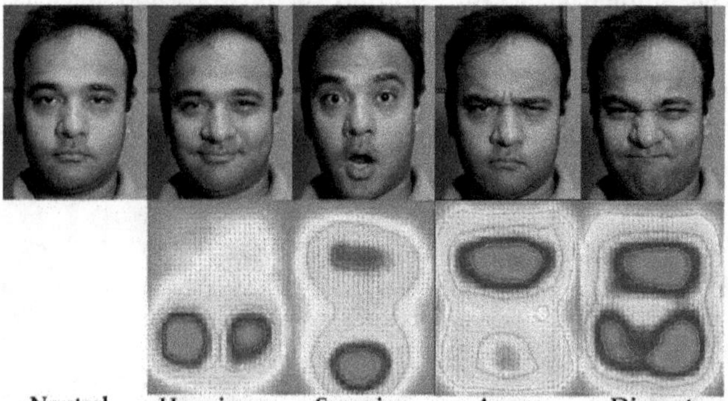

Neutral **Happiness** **Surprise** **Anger** **Disgust**

Used with permission of Irfan Essa.

Umberto Eco, an Italian semiotician, explained that we must realize that people can lie with signs. As he explained in his book, A *Theory of Semiotics* (1976:7):

Semiotics is concerned with everything that can be taken as a sign. A sign is everything which can be taken as significantly substituting for something else. This something else does not necessarily have to exist

> or to actually be somewhere at the moment in which a sign stands for it. Thus semiotics is in principle the discipline studying everything which can be used in order to lie. If something cannot be used to tell a lie, conversely it cannot be used to tell the truth; it cannot be used "to tell" at all.

People with dyed blonde hair are, in an innocent way, lying with signs. And there are countless other ways in which people lie with signs: cross-dressers, bald men who wear wigs, and so on. Because people can lie with signs, we have to recognize that some people have learned how to lie with their facial expressions, so we have to be careful when coming to conclusions about what people are like based on their facial expressions. Many white-collar criminals who have developed a means of looking honest (clean-cut, smiling, etc.) are lying with their facial expressions. Poker players are obsessed with facial expressions and the means of suppressing them. Being "poker-faced" is a means of not giving away, to the people one is playing poker with, any information about the quality of one's cards—what are known as "tells."

Gestures and Body Language

The nature of our bodies, the way we hold our bodies, and the gestures we use when talking with others also tell a good deal about us. In a chapter on "Body and Gestures" (in David Matsumoto, Mark G. Frank, and Hyi Sung Hwang, (Eds.) *Nonverbal Communication: Science and Application*), Matsumoto and Hwang offer the following insights into gestures (2013:75-76):

> Gestures are primarily hand movements (although they occur in head and facial movements as well) that are used basically for two purposes—to illustrate speech and convey verbal meaning. Gestures are interesting because they are a form of *embodied cognition;* that is, they are movements that express some kind of thought or the process of thinking.
>
> Gestures tend to be culture-specific and in some cases organization specific. Some are gender-specific, as well. In some cultures, people use many gestures when they speak while in other cultures, relatively few gestures are used.

The authors of the book list the way our physical characteristics convey information about us (2016: 5):

> By physical characteristics we mean the static physical appearance or smell of a person, including one's height and weight, skin color, hair, eyebrows, cheeks, chin, proportion of eyes, nose, and chin size as well as odors.

They also mention what they call "artifactual clues" like clothes, glasses, and jewelry and nonverbal behaviors such as (2016: 213: 6):

> The way a person looks, the way he or she moves, and how he or she sounds…transmitted through multiple nonverbal channels which include facial expressions, vocal cues, gestures, body postures, interpersonal distance, touching, and gaze.

We can see that there are many matters to consider when we look at people and try to determine something about their identity. Not only do we "scan" people we see when we are people watching, but we also do the same thing for people we see in videos, in films, at plays, on news programs, and everywhere else. Another important matter involves the styles and brands of clothes that people are wearing.

Brands of Clothes

The styles of our clothes and the brands of these clothes also are a means of establishing an identity. There are countless knock-offs of name-brand handbags, shoes, and many other things people wear or carry with them, so sometimes it is difficult to make accurate assessments of what kind of person we are looking at or dealing with. Knock-offs are a form of lying with signs adopted by people who like a certain style and brand of handbag or shoe but don't want to pay the price for the original versions of these items.

From a semiotic perspective, we can say that brands are signifiers that we use to help define ourselves to ourselves and others, and, to a certain degree, without being too reductionist, we can say that we *are* the brands we assemble to forge a public identity. We do this on our own or as members of groups that use style and brands to establish their identities. Brands, from Peirce's perspective, are icons that function as status symbols, among other things, especially when they are obvious—on our eyeglasses and sunglasses, watches, and so on.

The fact that our attachments to brands can change and that our sense of style is open to fashion currents suggests that identities based on brands are open to constant revision and change, which brings the question of postmodernism into the discussion. Indeed, it can be argued that postmodernism (or certain currents in postmodernism) questions the notion that a self is, in some way, a coherent construction and suggests that selves and our identities can be changed with little effort.

People's attachment to brands is often very strong. I had a friend, a prominent psychiatrist, whose attachment to Brooks Brothers was so strong, that he wore Brooks Brother's underwear, which are much more expensive than the more popular brands. Nobody knew he was wearing Brooks Brothers underwear except himself, which is an excellent example of brand loyalty and the role brands play in our sense of ourselves.

Figure 2.8: Brooks Brothers Logo.

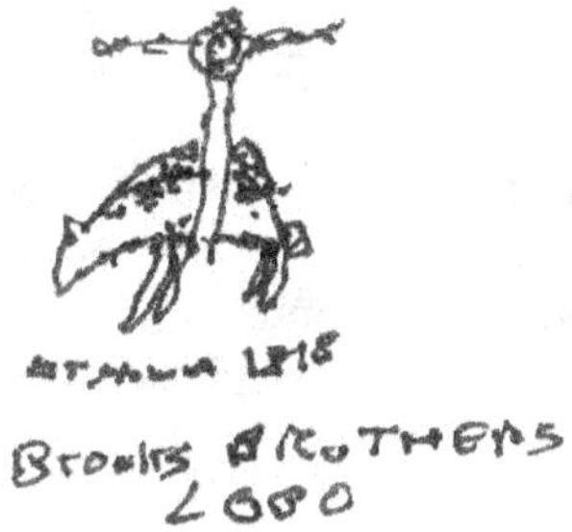

Drawing by the Author.

Women's Shoes

Women's shoes (and to some degree men's shoes) are an interesting topic to discuss since their psychological importance is much more significant than their function. The advertisement that follows, which is for Trump Towers, reflects on the anxiety that many women feel when it comes to purchasing a pair of shoes. And that is because shoes are not simply objects whose function, protecting our feet, is the most critical one. Shoes are connected to many aspects of our psyches of which we are generally unaware.

Figure 2.9: Shoe Purchasing Anxiety.

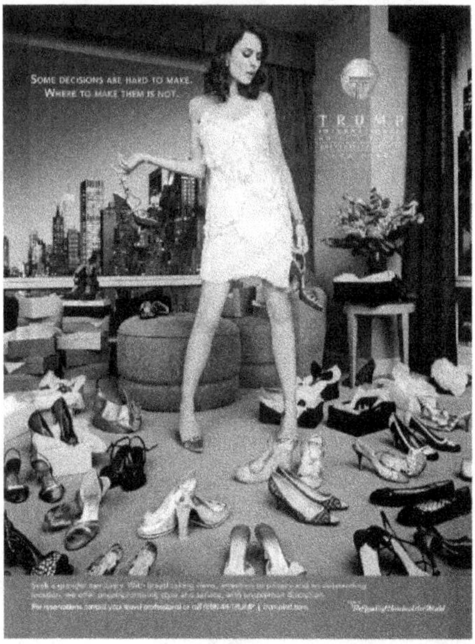

This advertisement demonstrates the anxiety that many women feel when purchasing shoes. For some women, such as Imelda Marcos, shoes are aesthetic objects to be collected because they are so beautiful, but for most women, they are objects to be worn but also to express something about the personality and taste (and age, in many cases) of the woman purchasing the shoes. The copy in this advertisement reads "Some decisions are hard to make. Where to make them is not." It is an advertisement for Trump towers but it shows the difficulties women often have in choosing the "right" pair of shoes. We see a woman surrounded by countless pairs of shoes that she has tried on and either didn't like any of them or couldn't decide on which she preferred.

Fetishism

In the fourth edition of the *Psychiatric Dictionary,* written by Leland E. Hinsie and Robert Jean Campbell, we find the following definition of fetish (1970: 300,301):

> Fetish (fe'tish). A fetish is a material object of any kind (idol, charm, talisman) which embodies mysterious and awesome qualities and from which supernatural aid may be expected. In psychiatry, the love object of the person who suffers from the perversion is called fetishism—usually a part of the body or some object belonging to or associated with the love object. The fetish replaces or substitutes for the love object, and although sexual activity with the love object may occur, gratification is possible only if the fetish is present or at least fantasized during such activity....The most common fetishes—shoes, long hair, earrings, undergarments, feet—are penis symbols or serve to avoid complete nudity of the female, and fetishism is thus considered to be a means of denying castration fears.

We can see from this definition that fetishes are much more complex than we might imagine and involve powerful forces in the human psyche. In Alyssa Siegel's "Shoe Obsession: Women and Their Shoes," published in *Psychology Tomorrow* we find insights into the way many women relate to their shoes (March 7, 2013):

> Flats, heels, boots, ballets, sandals, clogs, platforms, wedges, strappy, buckled, lace-ups, peep-toes, I love shoes, desire and lust after them. I feel my heart race when I look at shoes I am considering buying, feel a jolt of joy when I wear them the first time. I know that I need to have shoes like I know that I need to eat and breathe. Perhaps I wouldn't die if I had to wear the same drab pair of shoes for the rest of my life but some part of me would wilt and fade. Sometimes when I think about the things I would scramble to grab if my house were on fire, I think about

> my shoes. I feel pretty confident that I would make sure my dog and cat were safely out of harm's way first, but after that I would grab my shoes.

We see, from this example, that shoes play an important role in the psyches of women and Siegel describes how her heart races when she looks at shoes she's thinking of purchasing.

William A. Rossi has written a fascinating book that deals with sexuality and the foot, *The Sex Life of the Foot and Shoe,* that begins as follows (1976:1):

> [The} foot is an erotic organ and the shoe is its sexual covering. This is a reality as ancient as mankind, as contemporary as the Space Age. The human foot possesses a natural sexuality whose powers have borne remarkable influence on all peoples of all cultures through all history.

Rossi offers several points about the foot to support his argument. I offer a selection of some of the more interesting ones.

> [The foot is] one of the body's most sensitive tactile organs, possessing its own "sexual nerves"—and capable of the most intimate sensations in touching and being touched. (4).
>
> It [the foot] has played a major role in the evolution and development of many of the erogenous features of the human anatomy—buttocks, bosom, legs and thighs, abdomen, hips, etc. What we refer to as "the figure" or the voluptuous architecture of the body, owes much of its sensuous character to the foot, which was responsible for the upright posture that altered the entire anatomy. (4).
>
> The unusual structure of the human foot which made the upright posture possible, also made possible frontal human copulation, a coital position unique in all nature. (4.)
>
> Of all the known sex-related fetishes, those associated with the foot, toes, and shoes are by far the most common. (5).

This investigation of women's shoes teaches us several things: it offers some insights into the sexual significance of shoes for women, but it also shows that objects often have important social, psychoanalytic, and cultural meanings that we must be aware of. We can say that the more you know, the more you can see in all kinds of things—semiotically speaking in signs--that might seem to be trivial and unimportant.

Boxed Insert on Semiotics and Identity

Semiotics and Identity

Chris Arning

Semiotics and identity would seem to have a close nexus. On the one hand, the very definition of identity in the Collins English Dictionary (Collins, 2014: 967) is "the state of having unique identifying characteristics held by no other person or thing" or "the individual characteristic by which a person or thing is recognized." But what does semiotics have to say about identity? Which semiotic concepts most enrich our understanding of this vital concept?

We can start with Ferdinand de Saussure (1913), who declared in the *Course De Linguistique* that meaning is differential, not referential. For Saussure, language does not work via one-to-one correspondences between labels and things, rather meaning comes through *differences* between terms. At the most basic level, for instance, we can see that cat is a cat because it is NOT either a "mat" or a "dog." For Saussure, language does not work via one-to-one correspondences between labels and things, meaning comes through the network of differences between terms.

For example, as you can try yourself, it is hard to define the meaning of FATHER except in relation to and in terms of its difference from kinship terms, like MOTHER, DAUGHTER, SON, and so on. The implications of this for identity are stark. We work out who we ARE through who we are NOT. In defining national identity, for example, we define Britishness in contradistinction to Frenchness or Americanness. We find it difficult to define any in-groups to which we belong without any reference to an out-group.

IDENTITY AS ROOTED IN AN ORGANISM'S BIOSPHERE

The fundamental idea here is distilled into a provocative equation I = f (O) or *Identity is a Function of Otherness* debuted by commercial semiotician Thierry Mortier at the 2017 Semiofest conference and subsequently written up as a paper. (Mortier, 2019). This pithy equation is a leitmotif for this short article on identity since a notion of The Other is constitutive of identity both in the biological and cognitive cultural realms. Mortier writes that though identity comes from the Latin *idem*, meaning the "same;" in fact, it is only when we postulate a sense of separateness from others, or "alterity," that identity is activated as a meaningful concept. As Mortier writes (2019:6): "An organism that cannot differentiate itself from its environment cannot see itself as a separate organism." He adds, "Both identification and relative position are conditionals for the object's agency, in an attempt to ensure survival, which presupposes self-awareness in terms of knowing the limits of the own form (self) and its position in the environment" (Mortier, 2019: 15) thus "I=f(O) articulates a general mechanism that turns objects, bodies, and organisms into semiotic beings." (Mortier, 2019: 1).

Bio-semiotics (Deacon, 1997) and adjacent disciplines like cognitive science and cognitive linguistics show how our situatedness in the world is grounded in our embodiment, motor functions, and our sense of a proprioceptive, inner-outer orientation (Lakoff and Johnson, 1999). The fundamental nature of inside and outside is expressed in embodied metaphor and in our language.

Scholars such as Jamin Pelkey (2017) have even rooted the meaning of the symbol X in the body memory embedded in our physiology; in this case, he situates the "extreme" connotations of the X in the spreadeagle posture. What is palpable is that whilst the simplest single-cell organisms have a membrane that governs their lived reality, human beings affiliate via different levels of in and out-group separating inner and outer, friend or foe, through our status as social creatures. So, anthroposemiotics is rooted in biological distinction. Eminent bio-semiotician, Jesper Hoffmeyer states, summing up this idea: "Semiotics is in principle always connected with some kind of inside-outside interaction." (Hoffmeyer, 2007 quoted in Mortier, 2019: 2).

PERSONAL IDENTITY THROUGH HABIT FORMATION

But taking man as an organism in our environment, how do we become individuals? Indian icon Mahatma Gandhi once said that our thoughts become words, words become behaviors that become habits, and habits our values that then eventually become our destiny.

The American polymath and the forefather of semiotics Charles Sanders Peirce famously wrote that (Zeman (1977:22) a *"sign is something that stands to something for something in some respect or capacity."*

He defined a symbol as that sign which gained meaning through habit or convention, drawing a parallel with the way personal characteristics gradually accumulate around a person as they grow.

> "[...] the word or sign which man uses is the man himself. For, as the fact that every thought is a sign, taken in conjunction with the fact that life is a train of thought, proves that man is a sign; so, that every thought is an external sign, proves that man is an external sign. That is to say, the man and the external sign are identical, in the same sense in which the words homo and man are identical. Thus, my language is the sum total of myself; the man is the thought." (Peirce, 1932, CP 5.314).

Peirce saw human personality as a chain of signs that eventually form into a habit. We probably all resonate with the idea of loved ones becoming more "like themselves" as they age, as their views harden, their habits ossify and they become increasingly stubborn.

CULTURAL IDENTITY AS A FUNCTION OF BINARIES

If we return to that fundamental idea of I = f(O), this thought can be taken further into considering the realm of culture and how national, ethnic and racial identity sets are formed. As human beings, we define our identity through in vs. out-group behaviors.

Recent awareness-raising work around racism seeks to render "whiteness" conspicuous as a racial category since it tends to languish "unmarked" and taken for granted as a norm. Unmarked in this context borrows a linguistic concept originally devised by Roman Jakobson, who applied it to binaries in language: "every single constituent of any linguistic system" is really "built on…the presence of an attribute ("markedness") in contraposition to its absence ("unmarkedness"). (Zeruvabel, 2018 and Jakobson, 1987). Identities deemed different stand out, witness the "marked" nature of blackness vs. white within mainstream North American society.

In *Playing in the Dark: Whiteness and the Literary Imagination,* Toni Morrison (1992) adduces evidence to show we can read into the literature of 19th century American literature a dominant identity construction through ascribing hierarchical values to blackness and whiteness; that defines whiteness as innocence, individuality, heroism against a suppressed black, Other, freighted with negative values, just lurking under the surface. "Black slavery enriched the country's creative possibilities. For, in that construction of blackness and enslavement could be found not only the not-free but also, with the dramatic polarity created by skin color; the projection of the not-me." (Morrison, 1992: 36).

James Baldwin in his tract, *I Am Not Your Negro* (Baldwin, 2017) discussed the N word being an invention of white society that estranged them from black people, "it is entirely up to the American people whether or not they are going to face and deal with and embrace this stranger who they have maligned so long." (Baldwin; 2017:108). French deconstructionist Jacques Derrida would probably have argued that the Otherness is not a separation but a contagion and that one identity is always parasitic upon and contains a trace of The Other. Indeed, African American novelist and essayist Ralph Ellison, in his article *What would America be Like Without Blacks* (Ellison, 1994), argued that Black vernacular had inextricably suffused American dialect. Notwithstanding this, that the need to quarantine pristine whiteness from one drop of "miscegenating" black blood has been the great historical American obsession that shows the power of identity.

Readers might wonder why I have chosen the polemical topic of race. Well, they say, *"write about what you know."* As a mixed-race Briton, I grew up reflecting on a confusing upbringing. I grew up politically black but not culturally black (lacking the codes and proximity to Black-Caribbean cultural resources), which meant feeling white and not belonging within predominantly black environments and not being accepted (and subject to colorist discrimination) in white middle-class British society. I was caught in a double bind of not white enough or black enough to belong to EITHER. This lack of belonging propelled me to sample other cultures to escape the strictures of this binary. I lived in Spain and traveled around Latin America.

For me, the exuberance of Latin culture and the gamut of shades of brown into which I fit there felt like a contrast to a repressively exclusionary white middle-class English society. Later, a year spent living in Japan felt refreshing, partly because in that country all expatriates experience a certain blanket xenophobia regardless of their identity, and discrimination is primarily based on them being non-Japanese *gaijin* (foreigners). This felt the opposite of the rancor of "monoracism" an assiduous "policing" of my blackness I found in the Black British community and within the Caribbean. We can plot both all these identities on a semiotic square. A semiotic square is a key tool of semioticians of the Paris School developed by Algirdas Greimas, based on a logic square that sets out oppositional meanings (Floch: 2001: 20).

My reflection is that a dislocated identity resolves itself and attains a form of multifarious wholeness through navigating around these perceived binary opposites as shown below.

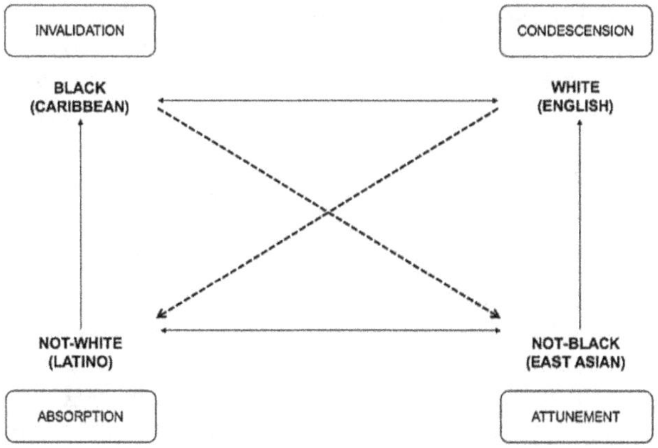

Diagram by Chris Arning

My identity moved around a semiotic square in response to feeling "Othered" in communities in which I sought belonging. This is a prime example of what Merja Bauters (2007) in her dissertation discussed as an 'updated image', coming about as a result of a certain reaction to emotional triggers and experiences that cause turmoil but then reassessment and become embodied as new habits. The idea of settled beliefs interrupted by perturbations to the organism that triggers a reconstitution of self on a new basis comes from Peirce. This mode of transformation is consistent with Anthony Giddens's notion of a "self-reflexive project" we introduce below.

Of course, my case is far from unique. British-Ghanaian journalist Afua Hirsch author of *Bri-tish* (2018), a meditation on race, identity, and belonging, argues that an unquestioned assumption that Britishness equals whiteness (based on an underlying colonial hierarchy) problematizes British identity for many people of color.

Chris Rojek writes about the Flexi-Brit of the multi-cultural 90s happy to identify with Britishness as an aggregation of cultural capital, (BBC's *Little Britain*) and tacit behavioral quirks, rather than anything that more narrowly defines Britishness in terms of ethnicity or myths of genealogy (e.g., Albion). He writes: "Britons may bear the imprimatur of nationality on their birth certificates and carry it around on their passports. But the kind of Britain to which they belong reflects articulation of various inflections of Britishness and strategic judgments about identity." (Rojek, 2007: 59). This flexibility tends to be accentuated for people of color.

RACE (LIKE IN LANGUAGE) AS A FLOATING SIGNIFIER

Of course, conceptions of race and identity are not static but they morph over time. Stuart Hall, British founder of cultural studies, took Saussure's insight on language and applied it to race: *What do I mean by a floating signifier? Well to put it crudely, race is one of those major concepts, which organize the great classificatory systems of difference, which operate...the argument that I want to make to you is that race works like a language. And signifiers refer to the systems and concepts of the classification of a culture to its making meaning practices. And those things gain their meaning, not because of what they contain in their essence, but in the shifting relations of difference, which they establish with other concepts and ideas in a signifying field.* (Hall, 1997: 6).

We can see this floating and shifting in defining mixed heritage. Across cultures, the way that people of mixed heritage are classified varies. In the USA, the "one drop of black blood" rule makes even a very light-skinned "high yella" person "black," but in Brazil, where no one really sees themselves as "black," the same person would be a grade of light coffee-colored. This shifting of race as a signifier also accounts for the shifting labelling of what has been seen as the fruits of miscegenation (particularly people who are of black-white origin) over the years, as shown in the semiotic square.

This idea of race as a floating signifier is a useful resource for thinking about identity, alongside the idea of Identity as a Function of otherness, marked binaries, and habit formation in personality.

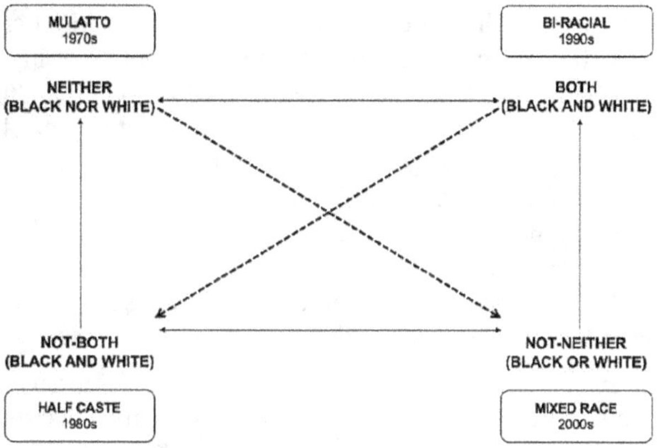

Diagram by Chris Arning

The mutability of racial categories in contemporary culture and race as a category demographically in its own right and a growing consciousness of heterogeneity and race agnosticism promises a cosmic race of future "signifiers." Far from feeling "half" of anything, many mixed-race people are endowed with two or more cultural heritages that mean that they are more accurately described as "double". Indeed, ideas such as "quantum identity" or "multiplex consciousness" have arisen to describe the ways in which aspects of identity come to the fore in different scenarios. This latter comes from what American writer W.E.B. DuBois refers to as a "double consciousness;" an amplified cultural perspective. This also allows what has been termed "code-switching" between cultural milieux.

IDENTITY, PERFORMATIVITY, AND TRANSFORMATION

In her seminal text, *Gender Trouble* (1990), Judith Butler challenged the attributes assigned to the feminine gender and naturalized female traits. What she argues is that gender to an extent, is a performance of a series of sustained acts. This whole concept of performativity is highly influential as a way to understand identity beyond gender. Whilst the gendered feminine have performance thrust upon them, performativity has now been ascribed to the ways in which more identity fluid generations more consciously "perform" identity. This brings up the vexed question of the extent to which identity performance can be genuine and the extent to which it must be grounded in innate cultural traits.

For instance, Performative Blackness, or what could be called "Black Cool," is a hugely saleable commodity in the consumer culture industry. It is associated for instance, with certain sub-cultural traits (i.e., Southern US, Jamaica patois, and Black British Vernacular). However, it can be easily and cynically packaged for white audiences; then risks veering into perpetuating stereotypes. Within hip-hop subcultures, the notion of "keeping it real" is vital. But in hip-hop, identity is also negotiated. Nitish Sharma (2010) in her sophisticated ethnographic study: *Hip-Hop Desis: South Asian Americans, Blackness and a Global Race Consciousness* showed how 2nd generation Indian-Americans rejected the "model minority" straitjacket and asserted their disgust at the socially conservative anti-black colorism of their parent's generation by embracing hip-hop culture but equally avoided seeking to be poor imitators of African American rappers by adopting the liminal position or label of self-identified "brown South Asian B-Boys."

Subcultures such as hip-hop make more palpable the performance aspect of identity and this performance can be used as a tool for transformation. Hip-hop, spoken word, and associated sub-cultures are sites where lyrical expression allows identity experimentation. This author has experienced composing performance poetry as a process whereby many selves are in dialogue and the result is a forging of stronger self-identity. It is no coincidence that performance poetry is inextricably linked with marginal identities. Collins and Bilge writing about *Intersectionality* contend (2017:121):

Spoken word poetry constitutes an important site where the content of youth identity narratives reflects an infusion of intersectionality's narratives off multiple identities...Spoken word becomes a place of healing from the injuries of varying combinations of forms of oppression.

This poetic impact is echoed in the work of cultural semiotician Yuri Lotman who, in *The Universe of the Mind*, introduces *auto-communication*, to describe the way poetry tends to be composed as a way of identifying oneself. He writes (1991:22) "while communicating with him/herself, the addresser inwardly reconstructs his/her essence, since the essence of a personality may be thought of as an individually set of socially significant codes, and this set changes during the act of communication." He adds (1992:20): *In the process of this auto-communication, the actual person is reformed and this process is connected with a very range of cultural functions, ranging from the sense of individual existence which in some types of culture is essential, to self-discovery.*

Anthony Giddens, in his book, *Modernity and Self Identity*, traces how the Self becomes "a reflexive project" as "modernity confronts the individual with a complex diversity of choices" (Giddens 1991, 107). This links very strongly with the notion of *bricolage* coined by structural anthropologist Lévi-Strauss, (1966) someone also very influential in semiotics. Bricolage can be defined as "re-combining available materials in a creative manner" and seems to define well the ways in which contemporary selfhood is carefully cultivated as a self-reflexive project for brand building benefit.

THE COMMODIFICATION AND FLATTENING OF IDENTITY

The "attention economy" places a premium on a need to stand out to grab attention. Arguably, the idea of personal branding is building a following through accentuating the characteristics one thinks will appeal to and connect with one's audience in order to capitalize upon it in terms of influence and thus capital. Matt Britton in his book *Youth Nation* (2015) anatomizes the disintermediating power of the internet that has ushered in a "democratization of celebrity." This started, arguably, with pop artist Andy Warhol who cultivated fame and celebrity through the notoriety of his art and life presciently claimed that everyone would be famous for 15 minutes. This has come to pass with legions of so-called Influencers on YouTube, Instagram, and TikTok vying for fame through identity. This breeds a culture where there is a motive to warp one's identity to appeal to an audience, accumulate followers, and monetize one's popularity.

Performativity seems to be playing an increasing role in the construction of public personas and curated celebrity in social media imagery too (e.g., cuteness in K-Pop idols). The perceived fakeness or inauthenticity of such portrayals is considered to be part of the digital hyperreal (Baudrillard, 1988). So, deception is a big part of circulated identities today and ties in with our increasing awareness of false information, simulacra, catfishing, and at its extremes, deep fakes too. These are identity constructions for external consumption.

In her book, *The Suspension of the Other,* Han Byung-Chul writes that the growing desire to create a unique identity is ultimately self-defeating (2018:19): "The compulsion to authenticity forces the I to produce itself. Authenticity is ultimately the self's neoliberal form of production; it makes every person the producer of themselves. The I as its own entrepreneur produces itself, performs itself, and offers itself as a commodity. Authenticity is a selling point." Later Chul adds (2018:28): "Diversity only permits differences that conform to the system; it constitutes an otherness that has been made consumable. And it perpetuates the Same more efficiently than uniformity does, for its apparent, superficial variety obscure the systemic violence of the Same. Variety and different options create the illusion of an otherness that, in reality, does not exist."

So, the ultimate teleology of this merry-go-round of identity is ultimately an even greater social conformity. This is hand in hand with the evidence presented by research company IPSOS in 2018 that the Gen Z cohort who are coming of age see binaries as increasingly being collapsed.

Eastern philosophies bring a new perspective by seeing identity as a fiction. In Buddhist phenomenology, the self is seen as a collection of aggregates or *skandas* or a collection of perceptions and mental formations that make up our lived consciousness but which do not constitute anything solid or real. A strong sense of individuation runs counter to the development of a calm and subtle mind. Attachment to views and a strong identity for Buddhists is a vice that only ingrains the poisons of delusion, craving, and aversion. A sense of hard identity falls away as the meditating mind deepens into a more embodied awareness, a more universal sense of humanity and discursive thought gradually withers away.

References

Baldwin, James. 2017. *I Am Not Your Negro.* London: Penguin Classic.

Baudrillard, Jean. 1988. "Simulacra and Simulations," in *Selected Writing.* Stanford: Stanford University Press.

Bauters, Merja. 2007. "Changes in Beer Labels and their Meaning: A Holistic Approach to the Semiosic Process". *International Semiotics Institute.*

Britton, Matt. 2015. *Youth Nation: Building Remarkable Brands in a Youth-Driven Culture.* London: Wiley Press.

Butler, Judith. 1990. *Gender Trouble: Feminism and the Subversion of Identity* New York: Routledge.

Byung-Chul, Han. 2018. *The Expulsion of the Other, Society Perception and Communication Today.* Cambridge: Polity Press.

Collins, Patricia and Sirma Bilge. 2016. *Intersectionality.* Cambridge: Polity Press.

Collins Dictionary. 2014. Glasgow: William Collins Sons & Co.

Deacon, Terence. 1997. *The Symbolic Species.* New York: W.W. Norton &Company.

Ehala, Martin. 2018. *Signs of Identity: The Anatomy of Belonging.* London: Routledge.

Ellison, Ralph. 1994. "What American Would be like Without Blacks," in *The Collected Essays of Ralph Ellison.* New York: Modern Library.

Floch, Jean-Marie. 2001. *Semiotics, Marketing, and Communication.* New York: Palgrave.

Hall, Stuart. 1997. "Race: The Floating Signifier." Media Education Foundation.

Hirsch, Afua. 2018. *Brit(ish): On Race, Identity, and* Belonging. New York: Vintage Press.

Hoffmeyer, Jesper. 2007. "Semiotic Scaffolding in Living Systems," in Barbieri, Marcello, (Ed.) *Introduction to Biosemiotics. The New Biological Synthesis* (149-166).

Giddens, Anthony. 1991. *Modernity and Self-identity.* London: Polity Press.

IPSOS THINKS. 2018. 'Gen Z Beyond Binaries'. https://thinks.ipsos-mori.com/introduction/.

Jakobson, Roman. 1987. *Language in Literature.* Cambridge: Harvard University Press; http://assets.press.princeton.edu/chapters/s11226.pdf.

Lakoff, George and Mark Johnson. 1999. *Philosophy in the Flesh: Embodied Mind and the Challenge to Western Thought.* Chicago: University of Chicago Press.

Lévi-Strauss, Claude. 1966. *The Savage Mind.* University of Chicago Press.

Lotman, Juri. 1991. *The Universe of the Mind: Semiotics Theory of Culture.* London: I.B.Taurus.

Morrison, Toni. 1992. *Playing in the Dark: Whiteness and the Literary Imagination.* Cambridge, MA: Harvard University Press.

Mortier, Thierry. 2020. 'I=f(O), Identity is a function of Otherness'. Unpublished, forthcoming.

Peirce, Charles. 1932. *The Collected Papers.* Harvard University Press.

Pelkey, Jamin. 2017. *The Semiotics of X.* London: Bloomsbury Academic Press.

Rojek, Chris 2007. *Brit-Myth: Who do the British think they are?* London: Reaktion Books.

Saussure, Ferdinand de. 1913/1966. *Course in General Linguistics.* New York: McGraw Hill.

Sharma, Nitasha Tamar. 2010. *Hip-Hop Desis: South Asian Americans, Blackness and a Global Race Consciousness.* Durham: Duke University Press.

Zeman, J.J. 1977. "Peirce's Theory of Signs," in Sebeok, T.A, (Ed.). *A Perfusion of Signs.* Bloomington: Indiana University Press.

Zeruvabel, Eviatar. 2018. *Taken for Granted: The Remarkable Power of the Unremarkable* Princeton, NJ: Princeton University Press.

Chapter 3
Sociological Aspects of Identity

> This book is about identity-seeking movements of modern society. It deals with such things as fashions, fads, poses, rituals, cultic movements, recreation heroes and celebrities, and crusades from the point of view of what they tell us about the identity search of a mass society. My view, briefly, is that a collective search is symptomatic of the fact that some modern social systems deprive people of the psychological "payoffs," the lack of which, expressed by terms such as alienation, meaninglessness, identity problem, motivates a mass groping for activities and symbols with which to restore or find a new identity. People grope because they do not really know what is wrong, especially when there is physical prosperity *yet* a sense of being cheated. When mass movements become concerned with identity, they develop certain characteristics such as "ego-screaming," concern with costume and self-ornamentation, style rebellion, concern with emotional gestures rather than practical effects, adulation of heroes, cultism, and the like, with which I shall deal. Such signs show that ordinary economic and political solutions are not what is wanted.
>
> Orrin E. Klapp. *Collective Search for Identity*

The term "sociological" is used in a broad sense here, covering many different aspects of our membership in groups, and the way where we were born and raised influences our sense of our identity, our demographic profiles, and related matters. Human beings are social animals and our identities are, to a considerable degree, shaped by our experiences in our families, in educational institutions, in organizations we belong to, in our religions, in our relations with others, and by what is called "national character."

Informal High School Groups and Identity

My students, in one of my classes on popular culture, started discussing what clubs they belonged to in high school. It turns out that high schools (at least those in California) had many informal groups to which students belonged, leading them to classify them in interesting ways. They mentioned the following:

Jocks
Cheer Leaders
Nerds
White Punks on Dope
Skateboarders
Preppies
Mexicans
Arty types
Brains
Queers

and any number of others whose names I cannot recall. What it shows is that there is a seemingly natural need for people to associate with others who are more or less like them and will give them support and standing. And identities. When I attended high school, in the late forties, we had clubs but they were connected to the school: putting out a yearbook, playing sports, being in a play, and so on. But there weren't the informal groups that my students talked about in my class. High school is a very difficult period for young people, who have to navigate complicated social relationships and who have to determine, at the ending of high school, what to do with themselves. For many people, going to college solves that problem for a while, but for those who do not go on to further their education, there is the matter of finding a job.

National Character and Identity

Geoffrey Gorer, a British anthropologist, offers some theories that explain how growing up in a country shapes our behavior. He discusses this in his book *The People of Great Russia: A Psychological Study.* He writes, in the Introduction to the book about the way cultures maintain themselves (1961: xxxix):

> If we accept the fact that all the peoples of the world are human, with the same physiology and the same psychological potentialities, whatever their present level of technological development, system of values, or political organization, and that all human beings are organized into societies with distinctive cultures, then all human beings and human societies can be studied, at least potentially, by scientific techniques which have been developed to these ends. Of these scientific techniques, social anthropology and whole-person psychology (including depth psychology and developmental data of ethology) are the most appropriate. Psychology has shown that in the life of any individual the process of learning is cumulative, so that early learning influences later learning; social anthropology has shown that culture is continuous over more than one generation, that the people who die are

> replaced by new members who have learned, by both conscious and unconscious processes, the values and customs appropriate to their culture and their position in it, or, in other words, their individual variation of the national character.

It is this fact, that national character is both influential and continual in our lives that helps us understand the influence of culture and society on individuals. Where we are born and raised makes a big difference in many aspects of our lives. For example, people who are born and raised in Boston have a Bostonian accent, which is quite different from the accents of people raised in Brooklyn or the Deep South. It also matters which section of Boston one grows up in. Bostonians from Beacon Hill (WASPS) are quite different from Bostonians from Roxbury and Dorchester (Jewish) who are also different from Bostonians from South Boston (Irish Catholics).

Bostonians are considered to be effete, perhaps because of their accents, or because of the aristocratic Protestant families that played a major role in Boston over the years, as the following poem suggests:

> Here's to the city of Boston,
> The home of the bean and the cod.
> Where the Cabots speak only to the Lowells,
> And the Lowells speak only to God.

The Cabots and Lowells were White Anglo-Saxon Protestants. At the same time, Boston always had a large number of Irish Catholics, who often were politically powerful, and Jews who were important in the creative arts and academic and intellectual areas. The Boston area is home to Harvard, the Massachusetts Institute of Technology, Boston University, Northeastern University, and many other colleges, which makes it a center of learning, and that has played a role in Boston's development.

Growing up in Boston means growing up in the United States, so American culture and pop culture also played a role in my development because countries all differ from one another in many respects. For example, the famous "British Breakfast" (which one sees when traveling in many countries) includes eggs, bacon or ham, beans, coffee or tea, toast, marmalade or jam, and so on while many French people have a coffee and croissant for breakfast.

Clotaire Rapaille, a French psychoanalyst, wrote a book in 2006 that helps us understand how countries differ. His book, *The Culture Code: An Ingenious Way to Understand Why People Around the World Live and Buy as They Do,* deals with what we understand to be national character. In his book, he suggests that children from the age of one to seven are "imprinted" by the places in which they grow up and this imprinting helps shape their behavior for the rest of their lives.

Figure 3.1: Clotaire Rapaille.

Drawing by the author.

He writes (2006: 21):

"Most of us imprint the meanings of the things most central to our lives by the age of seven. This is because emotion is the central force for children under the age of seven." He argues that three kinds of unconscious shape our behavior: a Freudian individual unconscious, a Jungian collective unconscious, and a cultural unconscious. This cultural unconscious represents the codes imprinted on us that shape our behavior. He explains the relationship that exists between codes and imprints (2006:11):

> An imprint and its Code are like a lock and its combination. If you have all the right numbers in the right sequence, you can open the lock. Doing so over a vast array of imprints has profound implications. It brings to us the answer to one of our most fundamental questions: why do we act the way we do? Understanding the Culture Code provides us with a remarkable new tool—a new set of glasses, if you will, with which to view ourselves and our behaviors. It changes the way we see everything around us. What's more, it confirms what we have always suspected is true—that, despite our common humanity, people around the world really *are* different. The Culture Code offers a way to understand how.

Rapaille enables us to understand the differences between Americans and people in other cultures. We have all have been imprinted by different codes that affect our behavior. Let me offer a comparison of American culture and European culture, which is where many Americans came from, that shows many of the differences between the two. Below is a chart I made that offers what we may consider being binary or polar opposites between America and Europe. It may be a bit reductionist but it also reflects clearly how different Americans are from Europeans and people from all other countries. Rapaille argues that people in every country are different from people in all other countries.

Table 3.1: Bipolar Oppositions between American and European Culture.

America	**Europe**
Nature	History
Forests	Cathedrals
The Cowboy	The Cavalier
The Frontier	Institutions
Freedom	Despotism
Innocence	Guilt
Hope	Memory
Willpower	Class Conflict
Individualism	Conformity
Agrarian	Industrial
Achievement	Ascription
Equality	Hierarchy
Common man and woman	Elites
Classless (all middle-class)	Class-bound
Nature foods	Gourmet foods
The Sacred	The Profane

Table by the Author.

We find the differences between Europe and American in Ralph Waldo Emerson's 1883 poem "America, My Country." Let me quote some lines from it:

America, My Country

Land without history, land lying all
In the plain daylight of the temperate zone,
Thy plain acts
Without exaggeration done in day;
Thy interests contested by their manifold good sense.
In their own clothes without the ornament
Of bannered army harnessed in uniform.
Land where—and 'tis in Europe counted a reproach
Where man asks questions for which man was made.
Land without nobility, or wigs, or debt,
No castles, no cathedrals, and no kings.
Land of the forest.

In the United States, we used to contrast ourselves, and to some extent still do so to this day, with Europe and its nobility, hierarchies, ancient institutions as reflected in its kings, castles, and cathedrals. We no longer are without debt and many aspects of European culture and other cultures have been brought to America by immigrants from these cultures, but it is reasonable to suggest that we see ourselves as new people in what political scientist Seymour Martin Lipset called the first new nation, which also means, in terms of this discussion of national character, a different nation.

Traits in America

These lists of traits were made by sociologist Lee Coleman. Coleman also isolated terms according to the historical period and found the following ones mentioned as characteristic of Americans for all periods.

Adaptability
Associational activity;
Constitutional government
Desire for peace and disbelief in war;
Distrust of strong government;
Dominance of women;
Emphasis on money-making;
Equality of all;
Freedom from the past;
Glorification of "the common man;"
Great power of the judiciary;
Humanitarianism and Philanthropy;
Individualism;
Ingenuity and invention.
Liberty, freedom, and independence;
Localism;
Love of size and bigness,
Missionary Spirit;
Mobility, migration and restlessness;
National self-consciousness and conceit;
Opportunity;
Optimism;
Party government and loyalty;
Political isolationism;
Practicality;
Sovereignty of the people via public opinion;
Spirit of the Pioneer and tradition of the frontier;
Widespread popular knowledge;
Worship of schooling and universal public educations

The next list shows characteristics that are not as widely held as the others but are prominently mentioned.

Dominance of the machine;
Emphasis on efficiency;
Emphasis on youth;

Energy, alertness incessant activity;
Freedom of relationships;
Gambling, speculation;
Glorification of labor;
Idealism, prosperity and High Standard of Living;
Mass activity;
Propertyism;
Protestantism, Puritanism, Calvinism;
Trial and error experimentation;

Coleman also isolated terms according to the historical period and found the following ones mentioned as characteristic of Americans for all periods.

Associational activity;
Belief in the equality of all as a fact and a right;
Democracy and belief and faith in it;
Disregard of Law and "direct action":
Emphasis on religion and its great influence on national life;
Freedom of the individual: an ideal and a fact;
Local government;
Practicality, Prosperity and general material well-being,
Puritanism,
Uniformity and Conformity.

Leo Coleman, "What is American? A Study of Alleged American Traits." *Social Forces,* Vol. XIX, No. 4, 1941. (Quoted by Francis L.K. Hsu, "American Core Values and National Character" in M. McGiffert, *The Character of Americans,* Homewood, IL.

As we can see from Coleman's lists, there are many traits of American national character that are still alive and well today. (That explains why de Tocqueville is still relevant, more than a hundred and fifty years after he wrote his *Democracy in America.*) And some are not. The various characteristics above represent a general consensus in the minds of large numbers of commentators on American society.

The point that Coleman makes is that there is a great diversity of opinion about American society and there is great diversity in American culture. It is possible to argue that the various traits discussed above spring from certain core beliefs and values. That is the contribution that Alexis de Tocqueville, a French traveler in the United States in the 1830s, made.

Democracy in America

Alexis de Tocqueville's *Democracy in America* suggests that equality is the central value from which other traits of the American personality spring. He writes (1956:26, but originally published in 1835):

> Amongst the novel objects that attracted my attention during my stay in the United States, nothing struck me more forcibly than the general condition of equality among the people. I readily discovered the prodigious influence which this primary fact exercises on the whole course of society; it gives a particular direction to public opinion, and a peculiar tenor to the laws; it imparts new maxims to the governing authorities, and peculiar habits to the governed.
> I soon perceived that the influence of this fact extends far beyond the political character and the laws of the country, and that it has no less empire over civil society than over the government; it creates opinions, gives birth to new sentiments, founds novel customs, and modifies whatever it does not produce.

Figure 3.2: Alexis de Tocqueville.

Drawing by the author.

What de Tocqueville offers us is what he believes to be the core from which our various personality traits, beliefs and practices spring. As he explains, he always comes back to equality when writing about American attitudes, institutions, and society. Later in the book, he will coin the term "individualism" and discuss the role of individualism in American society, a trait that is tied to equality.

Individualism

It is only in egalitarian societies, Tocqueville believes, that individualism can flourish, though there is also the danger of conformity and sheepish imitation in egalitarian societies. He writes in a chapter "Of Individualism in Democratic Societies," about the dangers of individualism if pushed to extremes. As he explains (1956:192-193):

> I have shown how it is that, in ages of equality, every man seeks for his opinions within himself; I am now to show how it is that, in the same ages, all his feelings are turned towards himself alone. *Individualism* is

> a novel expression, to which a novel idea has given birth. Our fathers were only acquainted with *égoisme* (selfishness). Selfishness is a passionate and exaggerated love of self, which leads a man to connect everything with himself and to prefer himself to everything in the world. Individualism is a mature and calm feeling, which disposes each member of the community to sever himself from the mass of his fellows, and to draw apart with his family and friends; so that, after he has thus formed a little circle of his own, he willingly leaves society at large to itself.

He goes on to suggest that individualism "saps the virtues of public life" but eventually it attacks all other aspects of public life and degenerates into selfishness, while in aristocratic countries everyone knows their forebears, and people feel bound to others in their societies. He concludes this discussion by pointing out that in egalitarian societies people feel they owe nothing to anyone else and don't expect anything from anyone else.

This suggests that in egalitarian societies, there is, necessarily, separation and alienation, as people find themselves confined to the solitudes of their own hearts. This analysis, though written almost two hundred years ago, seems remarkably accurate, for as the free institutions—read voluntary associations—that he thought would help us solve our alienation have atrophied and diminished in importance, we find, too often, we are alone and alienated. Now, as one social scientist put it, we "bowl alone." Our being alone and alienated, and suffering from various other afflictions, was exacerbated by the corona vaccine that forced us to remain home for long periods and only have virtual social relationships using Zoom, Skype, and other platforms.

Demographics is Destiny

Demographics is the statistical study of human populations and groupings, generally focusing on such things as age, gender, race, ethnicity, income level, and educational attainments. The government uses demographics in its decision making and marketing companies use it in targeting people for advertising campaigns. Marketers tend to see people in terms of groupings they make based on demographic information they have. For example, one research company, Claritas, has developed a typology of more than sixty different 'kinds of Americans," based on their purchasing preferences, with catchy names such as 01: Upper Crust, 07: Money and Brains, 67: Park Bench Seniors and 68: Bedrock America. On its website, it offers a description of itself made by Wikipedia:

> Claritas PRIZM Premier is a set of geo-demographic segments for the United States, developed by Claritas Inc., (which was owned under The

> Nielsen Company umbrella from 2009-2016). PRIZM Premier combines demographics, consumer behavior and geographic data for marketers. PRIZM Premier classifies every U.S. household into one of 68 consumer segments based on the household's purchasing preferences-

From a marketing perspective, as exemplified by Claritas, whatever commonalities found in American culture are unimportant and what is important are the 68 kinds of consumers.

The Four Lifestyles and American National Character

A British social-anthropologist, Mary Douglas, argues that in any modern country there are four "lifestyles" that shape people's behavior and identities. It is called grid-group theory and claims that while people may not recognize that they belong to a particular lifestyle, they do belong, and being a member of that lifestyle shapes much of their lives. The four lifestyles are: elitist, individualist, egalitarian, and fatalist. These four lifestyles are based upon the strength and weaknesses of two things: 1. the strength of group boundaries and rules and 2. the number of prescriptions. Social scientists Michael Thompson, Richard Ellis, and Aaron Wildavsky explain in their book, *Cultural Theory*, how the four cultures are formed (1990:6-7):

> Strong group boundaries coupled with minimal prescriptions produce social relations that are egalitarian....When an individual's social environment is characterized by strong group boundaries and binding prescriptions, the resulting social relations are hierarchical [sometimes known as elitist]....Individuals who are bounded by neither group incorporation nor prescribed roles inhabit an individualistic social context. In such an environment all boundaries arc provisional and subject to negotiation....People who find themselves subject to binding prescriptions and are excluded from group membership exemplify the fatalistic way of life. Fatalists are controlled from without.

The following table shows the four lifestyles and how they are related to grid-group theory.

Table 3.2: Grid-Group Theory Lifestyles.

Group Culture Lifestyle	Strength Boundaries	Number of Prescriptions
Hierarchists/Elitists	strong	numerous
Egalitarians	strong	few and weak
Individualists	weak	few and weak
Fatalists/Isolates	weak	numerous

Table by the Author

Douglas explains that although they are hostile to one another, these lifestyles form the basis of people's behavior and their consumer choices. As she writes in her essay "In Defence of Shopping" in Pasi Falk and Colin Campbell's *The Shopping Experience* (1997:19):

> Mutual hostility is the force that accounts for their stability. These four distinct lifestyles persist because they rest on incompatible organizational principles. Each culture is a way of organizing; each is predatory on the others for time and space and resources. It is hard for them to co-exist peacefully, and yet they must, for the survival of each is the guarantee of the survival of the others. Hostility keeps them going.

Douglas offers her theory of the four lifestyles, often manifested in consumption practices, to counter the theories of consumption that come from a framework based on individualist psychology. She argues that "What we learn from Douglas is that taste is culturally shaped and not based on an individual's personality." It is, then, our lifestyle group affiliations that shape our desires and our purchases, and ultimately, our identities.

When we purchase things, then, according to Douglas, we do so to show who we are by showing who we are not. That is why Douglas can claim that shopping is "agonistic." We want to demonstrate, she says, that we are not a member of any of the three other lifestyles and are not guided by their aesthetic standards. Douglas moves purchasing decisions from individual psychology to lifestyles. Modern societies may be characterized as being consumer societies and "consumer cultures" but, if Douglas is correct, there are not one but four consumer lifestyles and they are of major importance when it comes to such things as individuals making decisions about what brands to buy, which is one of the primary ways in which we shape and manifest our identities.

If we are branded selves, it is useful to know that our choice of brands is shaped, in large measure, by our lifestyles. What we learn from Douglas is that (1997:23) "cultural alignment is the strongest predictor of preferences in a wide variety of fields." It is, then, our lifestyle group affiliations that influence and shape our desires, our purchases, our politics, our choice of wives and husbands, our cars, and our identities.

And these lifestyles are connected to demographic matters such as the socio-economic class of the families in which we are raised, by our race, gender, nationality, and many other factors. You can think of lifestyles as being similar to what Freud called the unconscious—material in our minds of which we are unaware but which affects, in profound ways, our sense of who we are and our behavior. One interesting aspect of the impact of society on identity involves the matter of taste. Most people would argue that their taste is an individual matter based on their preferences, but there is reason to suggest this notion is incorrect. The French sociologist Pierre Bourdieu has written interesting things about taste.

Pierre Bourdieu and Personal Taste

Figure 3.3: Pierre Bourdieu.

Drawing by the Author.

Pierre Bourdieu writes, in *Sociology in Question* (1993:27):

> Sociology reveals that the idea of personal opinion (like the idea of personal taste) is an illusion. From this it is concluded that sociology is reductive, that it disenchants, that it demobilizes people by taking away all their illusions….If it is true that the idea of personal opinion itself is socially determined, that it is a product of history reproduced by education, that our opinions are determined, then it is better to know this; and if we have some chance of having personal opinions, it is perhaps on condition that we know our opinions are not spontaneously so.

Taste, Bourdieu explains, is connected to people's social class and their social class is reflected in their taste in music as well as other things. Bourdieu indicates how tastes change and writes (1993:108):

> I must indicate how *tastes* are defined. They emerge as choices among practices (sports, pastimes, etc.) and properties (furniture, hats, ties, books, pictures, spouses, etc.) through which *taste*, in the sense of the principles underlying these choices, manifest themselves. In order for there to be tastes, there have to be goods that are classified, as being in "good" or "bad" taste, "distinguished" or "vulgar"—classified and thereby classifying hierarchized and hierarchizing—and people endowed with principles of classification, tastes, that enable them to identify among those goods, those that suit them, that are "to their taste."

Taste, we see, is connected to social class, and taste manifests itself in our choices—including our choice of spouses. Bourdieu has explained that the idea of personal opinion and personal taste is an illusion and both are socially determined. Once we recognize this, we will be able to have some chance of understanding the source of our opinions and our personal taste. What we have learned in this chapter is that to a considerable degree, our identities and things we associate with identities such as our opinions and our taste are socially shaped, if not determined. We may be free to act as we choose but it is various imperatives operating in a society that determines what and how we choose everything from our underwear to our automobiles and our husbands and wives.

Boxed Insert on Sociology and Identity

Sociology and Identity

Dirk vom Lehn

Professor of Organisation and Practice

King's Business School, King's College London

Interactionist sociology considers "identity" as an intersubjective process. This perspective differs from prior theories describing "identity" as subjective and internally located. It has emerged from discussions in pragmatist philosophy and sociology arguing for a reflexive relationship between subject and object. Charles Horton Cooley (1864–1929), for example, introduced the notion of the "looking glass self", suggesting that people's sense of self results from how they believe they are seen by others (Ruiz-Junco and Brossard 2020). In a related way, another pragmatist philosopher, George Herbert Mead (1863–1931), suggests that people's self emerges from their ability to view themselves as objects of experience. As we act and interact in the social world, we internalize others' perspectives of us as our own perspective and use this internalization in our actions and interactions.

Both Cooley and Mead, therefore, consider communication and participation in society as critical for the construction of the self. Their analyses have informed the emergence of symbolic interactionism as a field of research where scholars explore the construction, negotiation and management of identity through communication and interaction (vom Lehn, Ruiz-Junco and Gibson 2021). Over the past few decades, symbolic interactionist research has studied issues like the experience of gender and race, the construction of identity in and through interaction with animals and ghosts and the ways in which the use of new technology influences the construction of a "terminal self" (Gottschalk 2018).

In a different way, Erving Goffman (1922–1982) investigated the impression people "give off" of themselves when interacting with others. He argues that people have a range of techniques at their disposal that they use to manage the impression they give of themselves depending on the situation in which they find themselves (Goffman 1959). Resulting from Goffman's work is the dramaturgical perspective in sociology that is used to investigate impression management and related issues in a wide range of social situations, including studies of the performance of barbershop singers, the interaction between the police and protestors, and the dramaturgy of online experiences (Edgley 2013).

Symbolic interactionism and the dramaturgical approach are two important perspectives amongst others that form the family of perspectives called "interactionism." Another perspective that is part of this family is ethnomethodology. Ethnomethodology originates in Harold Garfinkel's (1917–2011) analyses of contemporary scholarly debate and everyday life. In his research, Garfinkel highlighted the difference between sociological theories about the social organization of action and the actual organization of action.

For example, theory suggested that a person takes on the role or identity of a security warden for as long as they wear the warden's uniform and stand at the doors of a library. Garfinkel (2006/1948), however, argued that identity is ephemeral as it is continually and practically produced as the warden acts and interacts with other people at the library's doors. As Garfinkel further developed ethnomethodology, together with Harvey Sacks (1935–1975), he developed conversation analysis as a particular method to undertake ethnomethodological studies (vom Lehn 2014). Conversation analysts examine sequences of talk to reveal their organization, how one action is produced in light of an immediately prior, and how each action provides the context for each next action (Heritage 1984).

Conversation analysts have made an important contribution to discussions about identity through the development of membership categorization analysis. In one of his lectures, Sacks (1979) discusses the descriptor "hotrodder" as a category that teenagers use to gain autonomy from the world of adults who often disapprovingly look upon them. With this lecture, Sacks highlights the inadequacy of outgroup categorization, including categorizations of people produced by sociologists. Instead, he argues to study how people themselves as "members" use categorizations of themselves and others in interaction. It is key to understanding the conversation analytic approach that the researchers examine talk and interaction to reveal how members themselves use categories when interacting with others. Studies in membership categorization analysis have been undertaken in a wide range of settings, including in education, health, mediation, and policing (Hester 2016). In police interrogations or mediations, categories are used to share commonsense knowledge and thus lend particular statements legitimacy by saying that one does or does not belong to a particular category of people (Stokoe 2009). In this short box inset, I could only touch on the wide range of interactionist approaches to exploring identity. Although there is a variety of approaches in interactionism, they share a common concern with investigating identity as a social process.

References

Edgley, Charles. 2013. *The Drama of Social Life. A Dramatalogical Handbook.* London: Routledge.

Garfinkel, Harold. 2006/1948. *Seeing Sociologically.* Boulder/CO: Paradigm Publishers.

Gottschalk, Simon. 2018. *The Terminal Self: Everyday Life in Hypermodern Times.* Abingdon and New York: Routledge.

Heritage, John. 1984. *Garfinkel and Ethnomethodology.* Cambridge: Polity.

Hester, Stephen. 2016. *Descriptions of Deviance. Studies in Membership Categorization Analysis.* Odense: University of Southern Denmark.

Mead, George Herbert. 1967/1934. *Mind, Self, and Society From the Perspective of a Social Behaviorist.* Chicago: University of Chicago Press.

Ruiz-Junco, Natalia, and Baptiste Brossard, (Eds). 2020. *Updating Charles H. Cooley.* London and New York: Routledge.

Sacks, Harvey. 1979. "Hotrodder: A Revolutionary Category" in *Everyday Language. Studies in Ethnomethodology.* Edited by George Psathas. New York: Irvington Publishers, pp. 8-14.

Stokoe, Elizabeth. "'For the Benefit of the Tape': Formulating Embodied Conduct in Designedly Uni-Modal Recorded Police–Suspect Interrogations." *Journal of Pragmatics* 41, No. 10 (October 2009): 1887–1904. https://doi.org/10.1016/j.pragma.2008.09.015.

vom Lehn, Dirk. 2014. *Harold Garfinkel: The Creation and Development of Ethnomethodology.* Walnut Creek/CA: Left Coast Press.

vom Lehn, Dirk, Natalia Ruiz-Junco and Will Gibson. 2021. *The Routledge International Handbook of Interactionism.* Abingdon and New York: Routledge.

Chapter 4
Psychology and Identity

> I began to treasure the words which were my father's only bequest to me. "Always remember," he had said, "that there is no such thing as pure male or pure female. Some wear skirts and some wear pants but this is only a convention. Every man is stuffed with womanly characteristics, every woman is fraught with man. The gap between the powder-puff and the cavalry moustache appears wide, but it is really a hair's breadth.
>
> Nigel Dennis, *Cards of Identity*

> Look thou to character. Give thy thoughts no tongue,
> Nor any unproportion'd thought his act.
> Be thou familiar, but by no means vulgar:
> Those friends thou hast, and their adoption tried,
> Grapple them unto thy soul with hoops of steel;
> But do not dull thy palm with entertainment
> Of each new-hatch'd, unfledg'd comrade. Beware
> Of entrance to a quarrel; but being in,
> Bear't that Th' opposed may beware of thee.
> Give every man thine ear, but few thy voice;
> Take each man's censure, but reserve thy judgment
> Costly thy habit as thy purse can buy,
> But not expressed in fancy; rich, not gaudy;
> For the apparel oft proclaims the man,
> And they in France of the best rank and station
> Are most select and generous, chief in that,
> Neither a borrower nor a lender be;
> For loan oft loses both itself and friend,
> And borrowing dulls the edge of husbandry.
> This above all-- to thine own self be true,
> And it must follow, as the night the day,
> Thou canst not then be false to any man.
> Farewell. My blessing season this in thee!
>
> *Hamlet.* Act 1, Scene 3.

Some may argue that my previous chapter on sociology and identity offers an over-socialized view of people. It is worth keeping this in mind when we explore our next topic, the relationship between psychology and identity. And in some cases, psychopathology and identity.

A Primer on Freud and the Psyche

To understand what follows, let say something briefly about Freud's analysis of the psyche. He had one hypothesis which suggested that there were three levels of consciousness: consciousness, the preconscious or subconscious, and the unconscious. We can see these levels in my drawing of an iceberg.

Figure 4.1: Iceberg and the Psyche.

Drawing by the author.

We can see that the unconscious represents most of the psyche and the conscious is only the tip of the iceberg. The subconscious is the area just below the waves that we can dimly access but we cannot access the unconscious, which shapes much of our thinking and behavior. We are often unaware of things that enter our unconscious.

Freud had a second theory which suggests that there are three elements in the psyche that constantly interact with one another:

The Id:	our desires, wishes
The Ego	rationality, reality testing
The Superego	guilt, conscience, etc.

It is the ego that mediates between our desires ("I want it all now") and our consciences ("don't do it. You'll be sorry if you do.) Both the Id and the Superego can become depraved in certain circumstances, such as from trauma. If either the ego or superego is dominant, the person has psychological problems. Understanding these concepts is important to make sense of the discussion that follows.

Identification

Identification is a complicated matter, which begins in infancy and plays a significant role in our development. In his book, *An Elementary Textbook of*

Psychoanalysis Charles Brenner discusses the relation of the infant to his own body and then describes the process of identification (1974:41):

> Still another process which is dependent on experience and which is of very great significance in the development of the ego is what is called *identification* with the objects, usually persons, of the environment. By "identification" we mean the act or process of becoming like something or someone in one or several aspects of thought or behavior.

Children, adolescents, and adults often identify with sports heroes or with certain teams and show their identification by wearing a jersey of the team and the number of a star player. You see this when you watch football games and many people at the games are wearing team jerseys. Identification can move from fanship to fanaticism, as is the case of some of Donald Trump's followers, who identify with him in many respects to the point that it dominates their personalities, their politics, and their lives. In one interview I heard on the radio, one of his followers said, his voice full of emotion, "I'd give my life for him. He's our only hope." Identification plays a role in our search for a self and manifests itself in countless ways as we develop.

Brenner deals with the role of identification in social groups as follows (1974:124):

> There is an important connection between the superego and group psychology which Freud (1921) pointed out in a monograph on the subject. Certain groups at least are held together by virtue of the fact that each of the members of the group has introjected or identified with the same person, who is the leader of the group. The consequence of this identification is that the image of the leader becomes part of the superego of each member of the group. In other words, the various members of the group have in common certain superego elements. The will of the leader, his commands and precepts thus become the moral laws of his followers.

Brenner mentions Hitler and his followers and members of religious groups or sects as examples of this phenomenon. My next discussion, of the ideas of Erik Erikson, continues with this matter of identification and, more precisely, of identity.

Erik Erikson on Identity

Erik Erikson was an influential psychoanalyst who taught at Harvard University and wrote many books such as *Childhood and Society* and *Insight and Responsibility.* In the latter book, he offers some important insights about the matter of identity (1964:93):

> True identity...depends on the support which the young individual receives from the collective sense of identity characterizing the social groups significant to him: his class, his nation, his culture. Where historical and technological developments severely encroach upon deeply rooted or strongly emerging identities (i.e. agrarian, feudal, patrician) on a large scale, youth feels endangered individually and collectively, whereupon it becomes ready to support doctrines offering a total immersion in a synthetic identity (extreme nationalism, racism, or class consciousness) and a collective condemnation of a totally stereotyped enemy of the new identity. The fear of loss of identity which fosters such indoctrination contributes significantly to the righteousness and criminality which, under totalitarian conditions, becomes available for organized terror and for the establishment of major industries of extermination. Since conditions undermining a sense of identity also fixate older individuals on adolescent alternatives, a great number of adults fall in line or are paralyzed in their resistance.

It is the lack of support in fashioning an identity by a culture or society and the fear of the loss of an identity that generates the kind of anti-social behavior and acceptance of absurd ideas we find in contemporary America, especially in American politics.

Erikson summarizes his views on identity as follows (1964:95-96):

> The key problem of identity then, is (as the term connotes) the capacity of the ego to sustain sameness and continuity in the face of changing fate. But fate always combines changes in inner conditions, which are the result of ongoing life stages, and changes in the milieu, the historical situation. Identity connotes the resiliency of maintaining essential patterns in the processes of change. Thus, strange as it may seem, it takes a well-established identity to tolerate radical change, for the well-established identity has arranged itself around basic values which cultures have in common....Identity does not connote a closed inner system impervious to change, but rather a psychosocial process which preserves some essential features in the individual as well as his society.

So we must find a way to sustain our sameness in a world in which there is constant change and in which many people do not find the resources in their societies that help them to maintain a stable identity. In more modern terms, it could be suggested that what Erikson is discussing involves the matter of authenticity and avoiding what has been described as a “fractured” self.

Authenticity

One important aspect of psychology involves the matter of authenticity, defined in Dictionary.com as:

> Not false or copied; genuine; real: *an authentic antique.*
> Having an origin supported by unquestionable evidence; authenticated; verified: *an authentic document of the Middle Ages; an authentic work of the old master.*
>
> Representing one's true nature or beliefs; true to oneself or to the person identified: *a story told in the authentic voice of a Midwestern farmer; a senator's speech that sounded authentic.*
>
> Entitled to acceptance or belief because of agreement with known facts or experience; reliable; trustworthy: *an authentic report on poverty in Africa.*
>
> *Law.* Executed with all due formalities: *an authentic deed.*

You can see that there are many different aspects to authenticity. In terms of our interests, authenticity involves being real, not being fake or untrue to oneself. Authenticity is a problem because many people feel they are not "genuine" and not who they seem to be but are impostors. That is, they are pretending to be themselves but their personalities are not genuine and a true representation of who they really are. I can suggest that there are three levels of identity from a psychological perspective:

1. Our **personas,**
   Which means our masks to others.
2. Our **privatas,**
   Which is the self we can recognize
3. Our **privatassimas,**
   Which is who we really are, hidden from our consciousness, generally speaking

Our personas manifest themselves through the personalities we create for ourselves, which, linguistics shows us, are masks and are not authentic. The term "personality" is based on the Greek word, *persona* or mask. Our personalities are the way we present ourselves to others and, in many cases, we feel these personalities are not authentic and we are impostors, pretending to be one kind of person but really, as reflected in our privatissimas, being very different. Polonius tells us in *Hamlet,* "to thine own self be true," but that is more easily said than done, especially when we don't feel we have a true "self." Some theorists have described this situation, in which we don't know ourselves as a fractured self.

The Fractured (Borderline) Personality

This personality disorder has been called "the fractured self" and it can be best understood as an example of borderline personality disorder. This psychological status is described by George Simon as follows:

> Borderline personalities have a fractured and unstable sense of self and can exhibit a wide variety of high-risk behaviors, including extreme emotional volatility, self-injurious acts and gestures, and sometimes even breaks with reality. So helping folks with borderline personality disturbances achieve a more integrated, stable sense of self is a real challenge. Fortunately, with recent advances in both therapy techniques and medical interventions, the prognosis for helping borderline personalities lead healthier, happier lives has improved considerably.
>
> The term *borderline* is often misunderstood. Originally, the term was applied to individuals whose psychological functioning was thought to lie on the border between *neurosis* — a raging unconscious conflict between a person's primal urges, or *id*, and *superego*, or conscience, producing anxiety and resulting in various maladaptive symptoms — and *psychosis* — a state of impaired reality testing resulting from a breakdown of neurotic defenses. However, while some individuals with borderline syndrome can indeed experience transient psychotic episodes, most professionals these days don't conceptualize borderline personalities that way. Rather, most see the syndrome as the result of a failure of the person to successfully solidify a sense of self. Borderline personalities haven't been able to integrate various aspects of themselves well and therefore lack a solid sense of identity.
>
> https://counsellingresource.com/features/2016/12/05/borderline-personalities/

One might suggest that there is a spectrum of personality disorders from those with a weak grasp on their sense of self to those with serious problems and BPD or borderline personality disorder who need help from psychologists, psychoanalysts, or psychiatrists. It is estimated that about two percent of the American population or about three million people suffer from this problem.

Avatars

An Avatar is an image that people create to represent them on social media sites such as Facebook. What kinds of avatars do members create for themselves? Some are pictures or icons borrowed from internet archives, scanned from hardcopy, or taken from other digital sources. Users might edit or combine these pictures according to their particular tastes. Some artistic members create props from scratch, although this is a fairly rare--and envious--skill. The technical and artistic ability one demonstrates through personal avatars is an important source of self-esteem and social status.

People have a considerable amount of choice in deciding on what kind of an avatar they want to create to represent themselves on sites such as Facebook, and these avatars reflect a variety of psychological problems found in those who create their avatars. But even "normal" avatars are problematic and, according to an Australian psychiatrist, David Brunskill, destructive. In his article, "Social Media, Social Avatars and the Psyche: Is Facebook Good For Us?" which appeared in *Australian Psychiatry* 21(6), 527-532, there is an important discussion of the impact of Avatars on our psyches. I offer several selections from his article. They are found in Arthur Asa Berger, *Media and Communication Research Methods: An Introduction to Qualitative and Quantitative Methods.* 5th Edition. (2020).

> The way in which the human user represents the self in cyberspace is fascinating, complex and with respect to our human nature, ultimately revealing. In seeking to explore the phenomenon of self-representation online, the term "avatar is a key concept to recognize and understand....The term avatar has been firmly high jacked and expanded in definition to include one's personal manifestation in a virtual world—the image you create for yourself as well as the psychological character of persona you present to others. (2020:44).
>
> It has also been proposed that five psychological forces (Grandiosity, Narcissism, Darkness, Regression and Impulsivity) vie to assert themselves as the material from which the e-personality is built and that they—in a twenty-first-century confirmation of the Freudian id—cause a transformation (and fracture) and personality, known as the Net Effect. (2020: 43).
>
> The following observations have been made: going online results in a state of disinhibited and dissociated personhood and this state is the foundation on which a distinct e-personality has been described as a virtual whole which is greater than the sum of its parts and, despite not being real, is full of life and vitality, existing as it does alongside traditional offline personality, but with the liberating advantages of being unfettered by either old rules or the wider social contract. (2020: 42, 43).

What Brunskill calls "the net effect" is, in essence, a description of the impact that people's use of their avatars has on their psyches and personalities: grandiosity, narcissism, darkness, regression, and impulsivity. This list of psychological problems generated in people as a result of their use of avatars on Facebook is connected to what Erikson discussed in his analysis of the problems and pathologies of young people, and some older people. These problems arise when people don't have adequate support in society for a coherent, sustainable and positive identity. Developing and maintaining a sustainable identity may seem to be a problem individuals face but the problems many people have in finding support for a suitable identity has social and political consequences and for some theorists is socially constructed.

Boxed Insert on Psychoanalysis and Identity

Psychoanalysis and Identity

Nina Savelle-Rocklin

On a Columnar Self--
How ample to rely
In Tumult--or Extremity--
How good the Certainty

Emily Dickinson

Our culture uses the term "identity" interchangeably with that of the "self" and equates identity with aspects of the self that range from religion, ethnicity, profession, gender, age, socioeconomic status, body image, and more. From a psychoanalytic perspective, identity pertains to intrapsychic as well as interpersonal and social characteristics. I will now describe the origins of identity from various analytic perspectives, and then elucidate the contemporary view of identity.

Sigmund Freud mentioned the term "identity" only once, during an address to B'nai B'rith in which he referred to his "inner identity" as a Jew. Although he does not specifically use the word in his theories, his concept of the ego, which refers both to an aspect of the mind and a person's selfhood, is in line with the notion of identity.

Identity formation refers to the ways in which we come to define and view ourselves. Freud's view of human development is based on the idea that humans pass through five stages associated with the satisfaction of instinctual, biological needs. If there is unresolved conflict in any of the stages (oral, anal, phallic, latent, genital) fixations occur and a person will be stuck at that stage. For example, someone who does not resolve the oral phase might have an "oral fixation" and self-soothe by eating, drinking, or smoking. That person may later self-identify as a binge eater, an alcoholic, or a smoker.

According to Freud, personality is set by the age of five, a premise that was rejected by subsequent theorists.

Erik Erikson (1956, 1959) examined the concept of identity as it pertained to psychosocial development. His views depart from the classic psychoanalytic stance in that he believes that identity development involves not only intrapsychic (that which occurs within the mind) but also interpersonal and socio-cultural elements. He proposes that individuals develop according to achievements tied to the environment, a significant shift from Freud's theory that development is tied to instinctual forces. Erikson also believes that identity continues to grow and change throughout the lifespan. Erikson (1950) coined the term "identity crisis" as it referred to the experience of doubts, regression, and shifts in self-image that occur during adolescence. He thought that identity was tied to an individual's own sense of continuity and sameness as well as the concurrent experience of being perceived that same way by others.

As psychoanalysis continues to evolve from classical Freudian theory, Heinz Hartmann (1958) and others began distinguishing the "ego" from the "self" as a major feature of ego psychology. The ego was seen as an agency of the mind and the self represents the whole person. The goal of ego psychology is to strengthen the ego so it can withstand both internal and societal pressures and conflicts. Later theorists (Edith Jacobson, 1954, Otto Kernberg, 1967) note that people's subjective experience of themselves does not necessarily line up with their actual characteristics; thus "identity" is seen as a fluid construct.

This explains why one of my patients, a highly successful and award-winning composer, felt like a "failure" because he had not won an Oscar. No amount of external validation could change his perspective, which was in part motivated by an unconscious fear of success. His father was also a well-established composer and my patient resisted identifying as successful lest he create a sense of rivalry with his father. By working through these anxieties, he strengthened his ego and formed what Emily Dickinson referred to as a "columnar" self. This solid sense of self provides support for the way a column holds up a building, no matter what the exigencies of the internal or external world.

Heinz Lichtenstein later explored what he called the dilemma of human identity. He writes (1977:166): "Any definable identity requires that we perceive ourselves as objects, which means equating identity with the identity offered to us through social roles. But with this, we lose the feeling of identity as the pure actuality of being." The fundamental dilemma of identity is that those two experiences can never occur at the same time.

The self-psychology movement led by Heinz Kohut in the 1970s viewed the self as the core of a person's psychological make-up. From a self-psychological perspective, if a child is mirrored, soothed, and made to feel a kinship with others, that child develops a healthy sense of self as loved and lovable, and is able to maintain a consistent sense of self throughout life. When there are deficits in development, children do not develop a healthy sense of self. For individuals to develop a consistent sense of self and positive self-esteem, they need a transformative experience in analysis. Through the experience of being deeply understood by one's analyst, they mourn the past, heal unresolved grief, and create a new way of relating to themselves and to others. As a result, the "self" feels more cohesive and secure.

Psychoanalytic theories on identity formation may be disparate, yet share the basic conceptualization that a solid identity develops through a combination of internal and external pressures mediated by both the conscious and the unconscious mind.

In terms of a definition of identity, several features comprise a person's sense of identity. It is a way of defining ourselves by relationships to others, such as identifying as a parent, a friend, a partner, a child. Identity also involves that which we are born into, such as our ethnicity, and that which may be fluid, such as political affiliation and religion.

Akhtar and Samuel (1996) suggest that identity includes such characteristics as a realistic body image, self-sameness, consistent attitudes, and ethnicity. The idea of body image as an aspect of identity goes back to Freud's (1923) assertion that, "the ego is first and foremost a bodily ego" (27) meaning that our earliest sense of self is a body self. Self-sameness refers to relating to various others in more or less the same way. The opposite of self-sameness would be an identity shape-shifter, someone who acts differently with different people, becoming who they want him or her to be, rather than carrying an aspect of sameness to varied situations and relationships.

Having a consistent attitude means being able to behave in essentially the same way even when confronted with variance in situations, experiences, and relationships. In the film Runaway Bride, the main character played by Julia Roberts couldn't figure out how she liked her eggs. When she was engaged to a man who liked scrambled eggs, she liked scrambled eggs. Another fiancé liked his eggs poached, so she did too. It wasn't until she felt a sense of selfhood independent of others that she realized her preference was Eggs Benedict. Instead of being a chameleon in their views, people with consistent attitudes are able to hold onto their political ideas, interests, taste in food, music preferences, and so forth, while still being flexible. Ethnic identity refers to belonging to a community that has historical roots and has common cultural characteristics. An ethnic identity brings with it a sense of commonality with others of the same ethnicity, and thus familiarity. There is a "we" aspect to this view of identity and people feel a part of a greater social group with rules and ideals. They have a shared sense of how things are and should be, whether it's, "We don't eat pork" or, "We have huge weddings with 300 people" or, "We value education."

Identity may thus be understood as a construct of societal, relational and intrapsychic dimensions. The formation of an authentic identity is one of the ultimate goals of psychoanalysis, which examines how early experiences impact a person's sense of self and the world. The analytic perspective thus examines how unconscious factors contribute to identity formation. By making the unconscious conscious and working through unresolved past conflicts, people find freedom in the present and experience their authentic selves, their truest identities.

References:

Akhtar, S. and S. Samuel. 1996. "The Concept of Identity: Developmental Origins, Phenomenology, Clinical Relevance, and Measurement". *Harvard Review of Psychiatry*: Volume 3, Issue 5, p. 254-267.

Bohleber, W. 1992. "Identity and self. The importance of recent developmental studies for the psychoanalytic theory of the self". *Psyche - Journal for Psychoanalysis*, 46 (4): 336-365.

Freud, S. 1923. "The ego and the id," in J. Strachey (Ed. and Trans.), *The standard edition of the complete psychological works of Sigmund Freud*, Vol. XIX (1923-1925). London: Hogarth Press.

Freud S. "Address to the society of B'nai B'rith," in Strachey J, Ed. *Standard edition of the complete psychological works of Sigmund Freud*, Vol. XX. London: Hogarth, 1959:271-4.

Erikson, E.H. 1950. *Childhood and Society*. New York: Norton.

Erikson, E.H. 1956. "The problem of ego identity," in *Identity and the Life Cycle* New York International Universities Press, 1959: 104-164.

Erikson, E.H. 1959. *Identity and the Life Cycle: Psychological Issues Monograph*: I. New York: International Universities Press.

Hartmann, H. 1958. "Comments on the scientific aspects of psychoanalysis". *Psychoanalytic Study of the Child*, 11, 31-53.

Horowitz, M. 2014. *Identity and the New Psychoanalytic Explorations of Self-Organization*, Routledge, New York.

Jacobson, E. 1954. "The self and the object world: vicissitudes of their infantile cathexes and their influence on ideation and affective development". *Psychoanalytic Study of the Child*, 9, 75-127.

Kernberg, O. 1967. "Borderline personality organization". *Journal of the American Psychoanalytic Association*, 14: 641-685.

Kohut, H. 1971 *Analysis of the Self*. New York: International Universities Press.

Lichtenstein, H. 1963. "The Dilemma of Human Identity: Notes on Self Transformation, Self-Objectification, and Metamorphosis". *Journal of the American Psychoanalytic Association* 11: 173–223.

Lichtenstein, H. 1977. *The dilemma of human identity.* New York: Aronson.

Chapter 5
Marxism and Identity

> The ideas of the ruling class are, in every age, the ruling ideas: i.e., the class which is the dominant material force in society is at the same time the dominant intellectual force. The class which has the means of material production at its disposal, has control at the same time over the means of mental production.
>
> Karl Marx, *Selected Writings in sociology and social philosophy.* (T.B. Bottomore & M. Rubel, Eds. T.B. Bottomore, Transl.). New York: McGraw-Hill. 1964

> The history of all hitherto existing societies is the history of class struggles. Freeman and slave, patrician and plebeian, lord and serf, guild-master and journeyman, in a word oppressor and oppressed, stood in constant opposition to one another, carried on an uninterrupted, now hidden, now open, fight, a fight that each time ended either in a revolutionary reconstitution of society at large or in the common ruin of the contending classes.
>
> Karl Marx, *Selected Writings in Sociology and Social Philosophy.* (Transl. T.B. Bottomore). New York: McGraw-Hill. 1964.

> The economic structure of society always furnishes the real basis, starting from which we can alone work out the ultimate explanation of the whole superstructure of juridical and political institutions as well as of the religious, philosophical, and other ideas of a given historical period.
>
> Friedrich Engels, *Socialism: Utopian and Scientific,* in R. Tucker, Ed. *The Marx-Engels Reader.* New York: W.W. Norton. 1972

If class conflict is basic to society, as Marx argued, then it is reasonable to assume that for Marxists, identity is connected to one's class and to the ideas one has about oneself. These ideas, Marxists argue, are generated by the ruling classes and produce a false consciousness the working classes have about themselves and their possibilities. In bourgeois, capitalist societies, it is not too reductionist to argue that identity is based, in large part, on one's class: a member of the proletariat or the ruling classes and the conceptual ideologists who serve them and persuade them of the righteousness of their behavior.

Figure 5.1: Karl Marx.

Drawing by the Author

Alienated Proles

Marxists, of whom there are many varieties, argue that while capitalism can produce goods, it also generates alienation—a separation of the self that has negative consequences for both members of the proletariat or working classes but also for members of the ruling classes. Karl Marx wrote about this alienation as follows (1964: 169-170):

> The alienation of the worker from his product means not only that his labour becomes an object, takes on its own existence, but that it exists outside him, independently, and alien to him, and that it stands opposed to him as an autonomous power. The life which he has given to the object sets itself against him as an alien and hostile force.

This passage is found in Karl Marx, *Karl Marx, Selected Writings in Sociology and Social Philosophy.* (T.B. Bottomore & M. Rubel, Eds. T.B. Bottomore, transl.) New York: McGraw-Hill. 1964.

Figure 5.2: Fritz Pappenheim.

Drawing by the Author.

A Marxist theorist, Fritz Pappenheim, has a useful description of this alienation in his book *The Alienation of Modern Man.* He discusses the writings of Franz Kafka (1967:34):

> Man's alienation and his anonymous way of existing have been described with methodic and terrifying precision by Kafka, who wrote of himself: "I am separated from all things by a hollow space, and I do not even reach to its boundaries." The main characters in the novels *The Trial* and *The Castle* are completely depersonalized and reduced to mere masks. This loss of identity leads to a state of radical anonymity, which the author symbolizes by not using a name but merely a letter of the alphabet to refer to them.
>
> American novelists also have described man's fate of alienation and homelessness. We shall mention only Thomas Wolfe, who devotes much of his work to recording the painful experience of the uprooted man, the nostalgic exile and wanderer.

He also discusses Arthur Miller's *Death of a Salesman* which portrays its hero, Willy Loman, the "other-directed man" who strived to be popular and liked but remained "absolutely lonesome and irrelevant, forever dreaming that personality always wins the day."

The terms that Pappenheim uses to describe people living in a state of alienation—depersonalized, mere masks, radical anonymity, lonesome and irrelevant—are tied, Pappenheim suggests, directly to "the basic trends of our age," and, among other things, to technology, social structures, and politics. These phenomena are not the result of psychological problems but are structural and are connected to the social structures in which people live. We are, Marx argued, alienated from our work and that leads to alienation from ourselves and others.

Pappenheim quotes Marx on work and alienation. Marx writes that the worker (1967:91):

> Does not fulfill himself in his work but denies himself....He therefore only feels at home with himself away from his work while in work he feels estranged from himself. His work is not voluntary but imposed, *forced labor.* It is...not the satisfaction of a need but only a means to satisfy needs extraneous to it. Its alienated character is clearly shown by the fact that as soon as there is no physical or other compulsion, it is avoided like a plague.

Pappenheim admits that in contemporary societies, there are more possibilities for self-realization but concludes that we can only triumph over the alienation from which people suffer by developing economic systems and social structures that are not dominated by the commodity structure—a process that he argues will take many decades.

Lenin and the Need for Revolution

Vladimir Lenin argued that we cannot escape from alienation by peaceful means but only by having a revolution in which the members of the proletariat take control of the state. As he explains in *State and Revolution: The Experience of 1848-51*:

> The overthrow of bourgeois rule can be accomplished only by the proletariat, as the particular class, which, by the economic conditions of its existence, is being prepared for this work and is provided with the opportunity and the power to perform it....The doctrine of the class struggle, as applied by Marx to the question of the state and of the Socialist revolution, leads inevitably to the recognition of the *political rule* of the proletariat, of its dictatorship, *i.e.*, of a power shared with none and relying directly upon the armed force of the masses. The overthrow of the bourgeoisie is realisable only by the transformation of the proletariat into the *ruling class,* able to crush the inevitable and desperate resistance of the bourgeoisie, and to organize, for the new economic order, *all* the toiling and exploited masses.
>
> https://www.marxists.org/archive/lenin/works/1917/staterev/ch02.htm

Figure 5.3: Vladimir Lenin.

Drawing by the Author.

As many scholars have pointed out, once a dictatorship is created, it is difficult to escape from it, and the history of Russia after the revolution does not give confidence in the benevolence of the proletariat once it assumes command of a state. We must wonder—is the price of escaping from alienation worth the trauma and chaos involved in staging a revolution and establishing a society with repressive politics, with gulags, and with the murder of millions of people by leaders such as Stalin?

Some thinkers argue that alienation is a natural condition of mankind and that we find alienation in every society, regardless of its economic order. Thus, one finds alienation in capitalist countries and also in socialist countries because it is a natural phenomenon. What we have to do, it is argued, is find a way to minimize its negative effects of alienation, perhaps by establishing social democracies such as one finds in many Scandinavian countries or by facilitating community organizations, such as were found in the United States before people there started "bowling alone."

If psychoanalytic theory sees identity as connected to individuals and their life stories, Marxism sees identity as connected to their socio-economic class and, in essence, based on a binary opposition: ruling class or proletariat. Marx argues that society determines consciousness, not consciousness society, which means that our identities are shaped by the superstructures in our societies and they are shaped by the base, the economic system, and the class relations found in that system. That is not to say that Marxists are not aware of some of the basic components of identity such as race, religion, and gender, but they are not as important as class.

Erich Fromm on Marx

Marx's goal, according to Erich Fromm, is to free people from the bonds that bind them. As Fromm wrote, quoted in Irving Zeitlin's *Marxism: A Re-Examination* (1967:23):

> Marx's aim was the spiritual emancipation of man, of his liberation from the chains of economic determinism, or restituting him in his human wholeness, of enabling him to find unity and harmony with his fellow man and with nature. Marx's philosophy was, in secular, non-theistic language a new and radical step forward in the tradition of prophetic messianism; it was aimed at the full realization of individualism, the very aim which has guided Western thinking from the Renaissance and the Reformation fare into the nineteenth century.

Zeitlin points out that the young Marx focused on the problem of alienation and emancipation, which involved escaping from the capitalist mode of production and the binding nature of private property and the servitude which it engendered. One's identity, thus, is primarily connected to one's class and freedom is attained by class conflict and the elimination of classes, which then enables people to realize their true identities. Achieving this state is the goal of post-Marxism, which focuses not on class conflict but on the complexities of identity and the demographic elements that play such an important role in shaping identity.

We have to make a distinction between saying that the base determines the superstructure (vulgar Marxism) and that it helps shape the superstructure. That is because, as Marx pointed out, individuals do play a role in determining how societies evolve. But there can be little doubt that class is of fundamental importance in the way people perceive themselves and obtain an identity. And the arts play an important role in shaping people's consciousness.

As John Berger points out in *Ways of Seeing* (1972:86-87):

> The art of any period tends to serve the ideological interests of the ruling class. If we were simply saying that European art, between 1600 and 1900 served the interest of the successive ruling classes, all of whom depended in different ways on the new power of capital, we should not be saying anything very new. What is being proposed is a little more precise: that a way of seeing the world which was ultimately determined by new attitudes to property and exchange, found its visual expression in the oil painting and could not have found it in any other visual art form. Oil painting did to appearances what capital did to social relations. It reduced everything to the equality of objects.

We can expand Berger's notion of "art" to the media, popular culture, and all entertainments which work to mold public opinion and shape people's perceptions of their societies and themselves. When it is implicitly ideological, we can think of it as propaganda or, as it was known in Soviet Russia, Agitprop.

Michael Thompson, Richard Ellis, and Aaron Wildavsky explain, in *Cultural Theory* how things can be confusing in class societies (1990:149):

> Things are never as they seem in class societies, Marx tells us, because exploitation must be disguised for the social order to be sustained. Since rulers do not like to think of themselves as exploiters, benefiting unjustly from the labor of others, and the exploited must be kept ignorant of their subjection lest they revolt, the truth must be kept from both rulers and ruled alike....n Volume 3 of *Capital,* Marx voiced his belief that "all science would be superfluous if the manifest form and the essence of things directly coincided." Implicit in this statement, as G.A. Cohen has shown in a lovely appendix called "Karl Marx and the Withering Away of Social Science" is the belief that all social science would cease to be necessary in a socialist society, because socialism, unlike capitalism, would not be based on deception.

This deception is necessary to prevent the proletariat from rebelling and challenging the domination of the ruling classes. One reason the masses lack awareness of their status is that the domination of the ruling classes seems to be the natural order and is all-pervasive.

Figure 5.4: Antonio Gramsci.

Drawing by the Author.

Hegemonic Domination

Antonio Gramsci's theory of hegemonic domination is one explanation for the lack of revolutionary fervor in the masses. Raymond Williams explains hegemony as follows in his book *Marxism and Literature* (1977:109-110):

> For "hegemony" is a concept which at once includes and goes beyond two powerful earlier concepts, that of "culture" as a "whole social process," in which men define and shape their whole lives; and that of "ideology," in any of its Marxist senses, in which a system of meanings and values is the expression or projection of a particular class interest....It [hegemony] is a whole body of practices and expectations, over the whole of living: our senses and assignments of energy, our shaping perceptions of ourselves and our world. It is a lived system of meanings and values—constitutive and constituting—which as they are experienced as practices appear as reciprocally confirming. It thus constitutes a sense of reality for most people in society, a sense of absolute because experienced reality beyond which it is very difficult for most members of the society to move, in most areas of their lives.

People cannot move beyond their sense of reality and if they have nothing to compare their status and identities with, they are caught and will accept their status and identities as natural and thus universal.

When to Leave the Communist Party

In Nigel Dennis's *Cards of Identity,* he has a section called "Secret Agent" in which a priest, Father Orfe, discusses his monastery which was designed to accommodate fifty ex-Party (Communist Party) men who broke with the Party. As Orfe explains (1955:256):

> Each heretic believes that he alone broke precisely at the moment when the *eau-de-vie* of Communism changed to the ditch-water of absolutism. Those who broke before him he regards as renegades, those who broke after, as charlatans.

He identifies the problem that Utopian theories all eventually face: Dreams and schemes of paradise always, so it seems, turn into nightmares.

Boxed Insert on Marxism and Identity

Marxism and Identity

Christian Fuchs

Beyond Postmodernism: Cultural Materialism

Identity is a major concept in postmodern theory. What is often meant by it in this context are specific social relations and features having to do with gender, sexuality, ethnicity, origin, age, ability, origin, and class? Postmodernists often claim that Marx and Marxists reduce society and individuals to class and the economy and therefore speak of class reductionism and economic reductionism. In turn, postmodernists have however often neglected the analysis of class and capitalism and have advanced an identity politics reductionism while class inequalities have at the same time exploded.

A cultural materialist position as for example advanced by Raymond Williams (1977) or myself argues that the economic and the non-economic are identical and different at the same time (Fuchs 2020a, 2017). Social production is the foundation of all realms of society and has its origin in the economy. There is therefore an economic aspect of all realms of society. Production and reproduction exist everywhere in society. But at the same time, specific realms of society have their own emergent qualities that cannot be reduced to society. Non-economic realms sublate (*aufheben, Aufhebung*), as Hegel says, the economy, which means that they are based on and not reduceable to the economic realm. In respect to identity, this means that economic identity such as class in a class society shapes all aspects of society. All humans produce and do so socially in particular social relations. But class relations are mediated with other social and power relations, such as gender, racism, nationalism, etc.

Georg Wilhelm Friedrich Hegel's Dialectical Philosophy

In Karl Marx's theory, identity is not a major concept. There is however a meaning of identity in Marxist theory that is different from what postmodernists understand by it. And this meaning derives from Hegel's dialectical philosophy, by which Marx was heavily influenced, which is why he is often characterised as a left-wing Hegelian thinker. One of the most important and perhaps one of the most difficult philosophical books is Hegel's (2010) *Science of Logic*. The *Encyclopaedia Logic* is Hegel's (1991) further developed and more systematic version of the *Science of Logic*.

Building on Kant's notion of the thing-in-itself, Hegel understands identity as the "*abstract 'I'*" (Hegel 1991, §45), which means that when we speak of a human individual's identity we abstract from everything surrounding that individual and just focus on that single human being. Each human being has an individual identity, the self. Each individual is unique. Hegel also speaks of being-for-itself or immediacy. Identity is for Hegel the starting point of the dialectical process. A being-for-itself exists only in and through relation to another being. It is what Hegel calls being-for-another (Hegel 1991, §91). Hegel also speaks of contradiction and negation in this context. One human being is different from others but it also cannot exist without others, it, in fact, exists in and through other humans with which it stands in relations. And these relations are productive so that new qualities emerge from the relations between humans. Examples are a friendship that emerges from continuous interaction, a new project, a new social system, a new type of society, etc. In such transformations, the relation between humans is transformed, it is sublated (*aufgehoben, Aufhebung*), which means it is at the same time eliminated, transformed, and lifted to a new level. And in doing so, a new identity emerges that stands again in a relation to another being. The result of this process is that being is transformed and is dynamic: "Something becomes an other, but the other is itself a something, so it likewise becomes an other, and so on ad infinitum" (Hegel 1991, §93). Hegel's dialectic is a concept of how identity is transformed through relations that are contradictory, dynamic, and productive.

Marx's Dialectical Concept of Society and the Human Being

How did Marx use Hegel's dialectic and the notion of the identity? He applied Hegel's concept of the dialectic for constructing a critical theory of society. Marx argues that humans are social beings, they exist as individuals only in and through social relations and they produce inside such social relations. For Marx, there is a dialectic of the individual and society: "in his individual existence is at the same time a social being. [...] The individual *is the social being.* His manifestations of life--even if they may not appear in the direct form of *communal* manifestations of life carried out in association with others--*are* therefore an expression and confirmation of *social life*" (Marx 1844, 296, 299). Marx is a sociologist in that he argues that everything that exists in society is a social relation. The human being is not a monad but an individual that is a social being.

And the individual's social relations are productive, which means that humans produce and reproduce society and social relations. This is precisely what Marx means by a materialist understanding of society. "The individual is social and societal and society my *own* existence *is* social activity, and therefore that which I make of myself, I make of myself for society and with the consciousness of myself as a social being" (Marx 1844, 298).

The Dialectic of the Economic and the Non-Economic

Let us now come back to the question of how the economic and the non-economic are related. That human beings produce and reproduce society and social systems as well as features of society such as goods, services, decisions, meanings, worldviews, reputation, ideologies, etc. is the foundation of any society and social system. For Marx, this is the economic aspect of society. In class societies such as capitalism, the economic relations in which humans produce are class relations between owners and non-owners of private property. The distinction between the working class and the capitalist class derives from this distinction. The capitalist economy compels workers to produce commodities that they do not own in order to obtain a wage from which they can survive. The working class is humanity's largest group (Fuchs 2020a, chapter 7). The capitalist class possesses the vast majority of the world's wealth, but is just made up of 1 percent of the world population (Fuchs 2020a, chapter 7). Class relations shape the lives of all humans in contemporary world society.

Humans also enter into political and cultural relationships. These are also relations of production. In politics, we produce decisions. In culture, we produce meanings of the world. In a capitalist society, the logic of accumulation not just shapes the economy, but also the political system, where decision-power is accumulated, and the cultural system, where reputation is accumulated. The result of the logic of accumulation are inequalities. The identity of an individual is shaped by all the social relations they are part all, the totality of economic, political, and cultural relations.

Class relations are a necessary feature of the contemporary individual's life. Other social relations cannot be reduced to class relations but are always mediated by class relations.

Karl Marx was not an economic reductionist but advanced a dialectical critical theory of society that stresses the role of the human being as a social being, producing being and therefore of social relations, including class relations and other power relations, in society. Based on this foundation, Marx developed a whole critical theory of society that remains highly relevant in a twenty-first-century society that is shaped by the Internet, social media, big data, COVID-19, new forms of nationalism and fascism, etc. (see Fuchs 2021c, 2020b, 2020c, 2019, 2018). Today, in order to save the world from barbarism, we need a particular form of Marxist theory, namely humanist Marxism, and a particular form of socialist politics, namely socialist humanism (see Alderson and Spencer 2017; Fromm 1965; Fuchs 2021a, 2021b)

References

Alderson, David and Robert Spencer, (Eds). 2017. *For Humanism. Explorations in Theory and Politics.* London: Pluto Press.

Fromm, Erich, (Ed). 1965. *Socialist Humanism. An International Symposium.* Garden City, NY: Doubleday.

Fuchs, Christian. 2017. "Raymond Williams' Communicative Materialism". *European Journal of Cultural Studies* 20 (6): 744-762. DOI: https://doi.org/10.1177%2F1367549417732998

Fuchs, Christian. 2018. *Digital Demagogue: Authoritarian Capitalism in the Age of Trump and Twitter.* London: Pluto Press.

Fuchs, Christian. 2019. *Rereading Marx in the Age of Digital Capitalism.* London: Pluto Press.

Fuchs, Christian. 2020a. *Communication and Capitalism. A Critical Theory.* London: University of Westminster Press. DOI (open access book): https://doi.org/10.16997/book45

Fuchs, Christian. 2020b. *Marxism. Karl Marx's Fifteen Key Concepts for Cultural and Communication Studies. Key Ideas in Media & Cultural Studies Series.* New York: Routledge.

Fuchs, Christian. 2020c. *Nationalism on the Internet: Critical Theory and Ideology in the Age of Social Media and Fake News.* New York: Routledge.

Fuchs, Christian. 2021a. *Foundations of Critical Theory. Communication and Society Volume Two.* New York: Routledge.

Fuchs, Christian. 2021b. *Marxist Humanism and Communication Theory. Communication and Society Volume One.* New York: Routledge.

Fuchs, Christian. 2021c. *Social Media: A Critical Introduction.* London: Sage. Third English edition.

Hegel, Georg Wilhelm Friedrich. 1991. *The Encyclopaedia Logic (with the Zusätze). Part I of the Encyclopaedia of Philosophical Sciences with the Zusätze.* Indianapolis, IN: Hackett.

Hegel, Georg Wilhelm Friedrich. 2010. *The Science of Logic.* Cambridge: Cambridge University Press.

Marx, Karl. 1844. "Economic and Philosophic Manuscripts of 1844," in *Marx & Engels Collected Works (MECW) Volume 3,* 229-346. London: Lawrence & Wishart.

Williams, Raymond. 1977. *Marxism and Literature.* Oxford: Oxford University Press.

Part II:
Applications

Introduction to Part II

In the first part of this book, I discussed four theories that offer important insights into the nature of identity and some examples of how these theories explain certain aspects of identity. These theories or disciplines or sciences, whatever you wish to call them, are the core disciplines in an interdisciplinary field called cultural studies. The theory behind cultural studies is that it often takes more than one discipline or approach to best understand whatever topic is being investigated. In this part of the book, my focus will be on various topics that relate to identity and not on theoretical approaches to the subject. In the epigraph to this book, one of the characters in Nigel Dennis's *Cards of Identity* explains that everything in the world involves identity. Charles Sanders Peirce, one of the founding fathers of semiotics, argues that the universe is "perfused with signs" if it isn't made up entirely of signs. Semiotics, we see, is an imperialist science that can be used to explain everything. With these two passages in mind, we are in a position to investigate identity wherever we find it, which if Nigel Dennis is correct, is everywhere. Below is a diagram, which shows how this book has been structured.

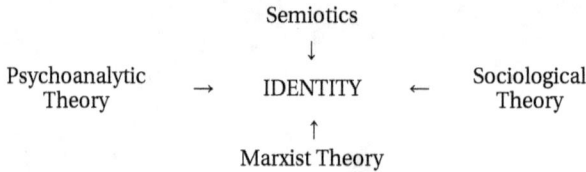

Semiotics
↓
Psychoanalytic Theory → IDENTITY ← Sociological Theory
↑
Marxist Theory

Semiotics	**Psychoanalysis**	**Sociology**	**Marxism**
de Saussure	Freud	Bourdieu	Marx
C.S. Peirce	Unconscious	Taste	Lenin
Sign	Id	Class	Pappenheim
Signifier	Ego	Gender	Revolution
Messages	Bipolar	Lifestyles	Ideology
Metaphor	Identification	National Character	Consciousness

Diagram by the Author.

These are some of the theorists and concepts that will play a role in the analyses that follow, as I investigate identity as it manifests itself in nationality, personality, occupation, group membership, race, religion, gender, socio-economic class, cuisine, fashion, and so on. The chapters in this section will be relatively brief because the focus will be quite narrow—but, I hope, revealing.

Chapter 6
Vodka and the Russian Psyche

Vodka plays an important role in Russian identity and is intimately connected with Russian character and life.

Figure 6.1: Vodka Brands.

Photo from Wikipedia

Hendrik Smith on Vodka in Russia

In Hendrick Smith's, *The Russians,* we read his analysis of how vodka shapes so much of Russian life (1976:120-121):

> The West has nothing equivalent to vodka, the way Russians drink it. Like corruption, vodka is one of the indispensable lubricants of Russian life. The mere mention of vodka starts Russians salivating and puts them in a mellow mood. It would take an encyclopedia to explain all the vodka lore from the gentle tap under the throat which signifies drinking to the scores of ditties Russians have invented to convey the message, "let's go drink." Vodka eases the tension of life. It helps people to get to know each other, for many a Russian will say that he cannot trust another man until they have drunk seriously together. Vodka drinking is invested with the symbolism of machismo....Among working men and peasants, vodka is so popular that the $4.80 half-liter bottle is better than cash for odd jobs.
>
> Those who have not been exposed to Russian drinking do not appreciate how hard Russians drink but travelers to Russia...have remarked about it for centuries. In 1639, Adam Orleans, who represented the Duke of Holstein's court in Moscow, observed that Russians "are more addicted

> to drunkenness than any nation in the world." In 1839, the Marquis de Custine, a French nobleman, picked up the Russian aphorism that "drinking is the joy of Russia." It still is, but this does not mean Russians are relaxed social imbibers. They know no moderation. Once the vodka bottle is uncorked, it must be finished....Russians drink essentially to obliterate themselves, to blot out the tedium of life, to warm themselves from the chilling winters, and they eagerly embrace the escapism it offers...Intoxication is the major factor in the majority of all crimes (90 percent of murders), accounts for more than half of all traffic accidents, figures in 63 percent of all accidental drownings.
>
> New York: Quadrangle/The New York Times Book Co.

Geoffrey Gorer on Swaddling

Smith's comments that the Russians know no moderation is worth investigating. Geoffrey Gorer, an anthropologist, and John Rickman, a psychoanalyst, wrote a book, *The People of Great Russia: a Psychological Study that* helps explain Russian behavior relative to vodka and related matters. Gorer discusses the practice of swaddling infants and offers an interesting hypothesis (1962:97-98):

> From the day of its birth onwards the baby is tightly swaddled in long strings of material holding its legs straight and its arms down by its sides. They do this because they believe it protects the baby from harming itself and keep babies swaddled for around nine months.

Gorer offers a hypothesis about this swaddling, which is that Russian babies who are swaddled feel intense and unassuaged rage at being constrained. This is alternated, over their first nine months, by a complete lack of restraint when they are loosened from their restraint. Later in their childhood, they experience few restraints.

So Russian babies experience, Gorer explains, both restraint without gratifications and then gratifications without restraint in their earliest months. This pattern informs Russian attitudes towards food and drink and many other things. They value maximum gratifications (1962:139):

> What Russians value are not minimum gratifications—enough to get along with—but maximum total gratifications—orgiastic feasts, prolonged drinking bouts, high frequency of copulation, and so on.

Gorer speculates that the drinking by the Russians reflects an unconscious search for absolution that is connected to their early experiences with the Russian Orthodox Church. We can surmise, then, that the way Russian children are raised, even if they aren't swaddled, shapes their behavior when they become adults. They alternate between opposites: abstention and overindulgence, starvation, and feasting. Quite likely, their religious beliefs add to their problems. In Freudian terms, they are dominated either by their Ids or their Superegos, because their Egos do not have enough power to restrain the two competing forces in the Russian psyche. Gorer's theories are quite controversial but they do seem to explain important aspects of the Russian character.

Chapter 7

Donald Trump:

A Study in Mendacious Irony

It is rather ironic, if you think about it, that followers of Donald Trump always praised him by saying "He Tells It Like It Is," while it is estimated that he told more than 30,000 lies in the period before his election and his presidency.

Figure 7.1: Trump at Rally.

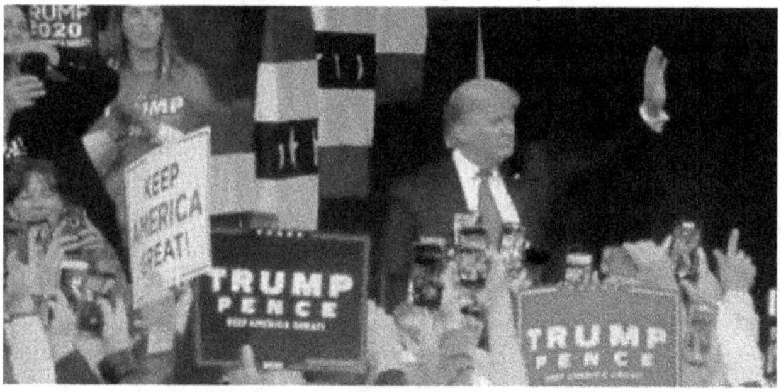

Photo by the Author from Television Coverage.

Trump as an Ironist

He bragged that he was immensely wealthy and, being a successful businessman, knew how to run a company and a country. In truth, he was not successful at all and ended up filing for bankruptcy many times. And his administration, which he described as "running like a well-oiled machine," was chaotic and dysfunctional. Trump has serious psychological problems and has been diagnosed as a "malignant narcissist," whose basic concern was being in the public eye and being admired by his followers, his notorious "base." He didn't find being president interesting but loved holding rallies at which he was the center of attention. He held around 650 rallies in the course of his five years in the public eye: before the 2016 election, during his presidency, and in the 2020 pre-election period.

Perhaps the greatest irony occurred when he spurred his followers on to invade Congress in a futile but destructive attempt to prevent Joe Biden from being certified as the winner of the 2020 election. We have here Trump using his followers to attack the government he led. It is quite likely that Trump ran for President as a publicity stunt, never dreaming he could win. That win led to what is widely described as the worst presidency in American history.

Trump as an Impostor

I would like to suggest another idea that will help us understand Trump and that involves his being an impostor. We do not know, as I write this, how wealthy Trump is, but we know he owes around four hundred million dollars to banks. Some writers have even suggested he is an asset of the Russian government and is a Russian agent, though he may not recognize that this is the case. But he may.

In 2005 I published a cultural studies murder mystery, *Mistake in Identity* (AltaMira Press). It involved a group of cultural studies professors and theorists who were about to take a cruise from San Francisco when the leader of the group was murdered. The victim, Marshall McInnis (read McLuhan), had gathered the professors together and the theory was that they would each write a chapter for a book on identity that McInnis would edit. As a result of the murder, a detective on the San Francisco Police force, Inspector Solomon Hunter, and his assistant Sergeant Talcott Weems, were assigned to the case and took the cruise so they could find the murderer.

At one point in the cruise, Hunter had a conversation with one of the scholars, Sigfried Duerfklein, a professor of psychiatry at the University of Vienna, about Duerfklein's theory about impostors. When Inspector asks Duerfklein about his theory, he replies (2005:110-111):

> My theories really bother my colleagues because they tend to look at human beings in aggregates, as members of society or some class or culture or sub-culture. So they can talk about things like behavior in crowds or American identity—whatever that might be—or various ideological positions, that still deal with large groups of people—women, gays, people of color, the proletariat....My focus, since I have a psychoanalytic approach to things, deals with individuals and how they achieve their identities. Or don't achieve them, since many people... are pretenders to an identity.
>
> You must remember that the term 'personality is based on the Latin root 'persona' which means mask. So our personalities are, it can be said, masks that we create to deal with others in social situations. You might contrast one's personality with what might be called one's character or 'self,' one's true being. What I argue, based on my work with numerous patients, is that many people never grow up, never cast off immature notions and fantasies of what it means to be an adult, never achieve coherence and continuity in their sense of themselves, so what you get,

> ultimately, is a fake person, a simulation, a fraud. And these people can't help themselves because they don't even recognize that they are impostors. They've devoted all their energy to fooling others and they end up also fooling themselves.
>
> What did Socrates tell people to do? 'Know thyself,' he said. It isn't easy to do. Also, these impostors suffer from a kind of amnesia, especially about their childhoods when many of the foundations for their identities were established and their adolescent periods, when they were searching desperately for acceptable identities. They forget who they were, so they are condemned to continually creating new characters for themselves.

Trump's niece, who has a Ph.D. in psychology, has described Trump's childhood and adolescence in countless interviews on television and argues that Trump's father is responsible, in large measure, for Trump becoming the basket case of psychopathologies he is.

A Psychoanalyst on Trump

A psychoanalyst, Nina Savelle Rocklin, describes him as follows, in my book, published by Peter Lang, *Three Tropes on Trump* (2019:92):

> Trump's predilection for lashing out against perceived slights, his vituperative and personal attacks on anyone who disagrees with him, his self-aggrandizing proclamations and inflated assessments of his accomplishments appear to fit all nine criteria of Narcissistic Personality Disorder as presented in *The Diagnostic and Statistical Manual of Mental Health Disorders* (5th ed.).

She lists some of his characteristics: a grandiose sense of self-importance, a preoccupation with fantasies of unlimited success, a belief that he is special, a need for excessive admiration, a very strong sense of entitlement, being exploitative of others, a lack of empathy, being envious of others, showing arrogant and haughty behavior.

Hillary Clinton attacked Trump during the 2016 presidential campaign for not having the temperament to be president and he insisted he did and was calm, cool, and collected. She was, history shows, correct and American society and politics were subjected to four years of his raging against others, insulting countless numbers of people, and lying many times every day in his speeches, his acrimonious relations with the press, and his countless incendiary tweets.

Many commentators have described Trump as being racist, anti-Semitic, authoritarian, anti-Muslim, and sympathetic with White Supremacist and neo-fascist groups. He has many millions of followers, who refuse to admit that Joe

Biden was elected in a fair election and an unknown number of followers—American terrorists who are willing to attack American institutions and have threatened American politicians.

Trump's Tweets

Trump's more than 20,000 tweets were analyzed by Professor Michael Humphrey, who teaches journalism at Colorado State University. He offers the following analysis of their contents (in *The Conversation* of Feb. 8, 2021), pointing out that Trump was a storytelling president:

> Storytelling in general is common among effective politicians, but Trump's effort appears to have built a high level of loyalty, diverted attention away from negative topics and generally set the agenda for what the American public was discussing. Others have looked at this aspect of Trump's appeal, examining specific stories throughout his presidency, his style of storytelling and even the rhetorical components of his populist narrative....Donald Trump knew how to tell a story – his own.
>
> There were five main themes, which appeared regularly – often all in one day:
>
> 1. The true version of the United States is beset with invaders;
> 2. Real Americans can see this;
> 3. I (Trump) am uniquely qualified to stop this invasion;
> 4. The establishment and its agents are hindering me;
> 5. The U.S. is in mortal danger because of this.
>
> Taken together over time, this formed an overall story structure that I summarize this way: "The establishment is stopping me from protecting you against invaders." The elements were flexible. "The establishment" could be anyone--Democrats, the NFL, a media outlet, a corporation and even Vice President Mike Pence. "The invaders" were China, the coronavirus that first emerged there, people crossing the U.S.-Mexico border or Black Lives Matter protesters. But the structure never changed: There was a danger to the nation, Trump was uniquely able to protect America and he was righteously supported by "real" Americans.

The irony of an impostor leading "real" Americans should not be lost on us. What we learn from Humphrey was that Trump used the power of narratives to create what can best be described as a cult following in many Americans, including Republican members of the House of Representatives and the Senate. Whether the Trump followers found in Trump someone who reflected their beliefs and ideologies or whether he "infected" his followers with his beliefs remains to be answered definitively. Trump now only refers to himself as the forty-fifth president of the United States and, refuses to admit he lost the election, a typically egregious example of his being an impostor. He has spent his life deluding others and now has succeeded (perhaps his only success since he became president) in deluding himself.

Chapter 8

Fashion and Identity: The Broadway Riders

Fashion plays an important role for us in establishing our identities. I have already discussed the matter of how brands of clothes, eyeglasses, shoes, and other objects help create what I call a "branded self." The advertisement found below is useful to us because it shows a motorcyclist in a full "uniform," and it is the clothing that motorcyclists wear that is crucial to my analysis. The advertisement has an enormous amount of copy which suggests that people reading this advertisement are interested in technological matters relating to owning, riding, and maintaining motorcycles.

Figure 8.1: Motorcycle Advertisement.

This advertisement shows a motorcycle rider in typical gear, with a helmet, leather jacket, and boots. It also had an enormous amount of copy in it for those wanting detailed information about the product it is selling.

Fashion and Identity

Ruth Rubinstein, a professor of sociology at the Fashion Institute of Technology, discusses the role fashion plays in constructing an identity in her semiotically informed book, *Dress Codes: Meanings and Messages in American Culture.* As she explains (1995:47-48):

> Because clothing signs identify expected role behavior, their significance is not limited to the specific situational context. The attributes of a clothing sign are relevant and carry weight beyond the boundaries of front-stage performance. They also enable individuals to *fabricate* an identity. By wearing the appropriate attire, a person can convince others that he or she has the special qualities and skills the clothing signifies....Believability concerning a particular identity depends on coherence between the impression one gives (a conscious effort to communicate a certain image) and the information one "gives off."

What we learn from Rubinstein is that clothing (in semiotic parlance, signs) plays an important role in the way we create our identities and we can use our clothing to convince others that we have a certain identity. We must keep in mind what Umberto Eco taught us about signs: they can be used to lie. This brings us to the primary subject of our investigation, a group described by Orrin Klapp in his book, *Collective Search for Identity* as "The Broadway Riders."

The Broadway Riders

The styles and brands of the clothes we wear send messages to others about what kind of person we are or claim to be. People scan everything we wear for clues about our taste and status. Some wealthy people dress down—disguising their status—while others dress up, pretending to have a different, more elevated status. So we have to be careful when we analyze clothes to make sure we are not being led astray by poseurs.

In his book, *Collective Search for Identity,* sociologist Orrin Klapp discusses a southern California gang called the Broadway Riders, in his discussion of group poseurs. He writes (1969:103):

> An odd example of group-supported pose is found in a southern California gang called the Broadway Riders—motorcyclists *without motorcycles.* They affect the style of better-known motorcycle gangs such as the Hell's Angels—black leather jackets, tight pants, boots, long hair, unkempt beards, chains, buckles, sheath knives protruding from boots, slit ear and earring, and so on—but the makeup of this interesting group consists of youths who, for one reason or another...cannot manage to

obtain a vehicle. The manager of a motorcycle shop, who knows them well, says:

> It gives them the position of being tough, to dress like them and be associated with their reputation; yet most aren't really tough at all. They hang around pizza parlors having nothing to do but discuss their exploits and their pseudo-motorcycles.

The Broadway Riders are an example of the way members of a group can support one another in pretending to have a certain identity. Members of such groups identify with a group they are imitating because of the social and psychological gratifications they obtain by pretending to be members of a group they imitate. Klapp sees this behavior as an example of a desire, found in many people, to escape from themselves, to become someone else, which to my mind is an example of their being impostors—a role that suggests that for one reason or another, because they lack social or economic capital, their real identities are not satisfactory.

Chapter 9

LGBTQIA+ and Gender Identity

The letters above stand for Lesbian, Gay, Bisexual, Transgender, Queer / Questioning, Intersexual, Asexual / Aromantic, and other identities in Queerness—all of which are possibilities in non-binary gender identities.

Non-Binary

It was Ferdinand de Saussure, one of the founding fathers of semiotics, who explained that binary oppositions shape our understanding of concepts and this phenomenon is built into the nature of language. Signs have meaning, he explained, because of relationships among them, and the basic relationship is oppositional. "In language there are only differences," according to Saussure (1915/1966:120). He added (1915/1966:117) "Concepts are purely differential and defined not by their positive content but negatively by their relations with the other terms of the system."

It is not their content that determine the meaning of concepts, but their "relations" in some kind of a system. The "most precise characteristic" of these concepts "is in being what the others are not" (1915/1966:117) or binary oppositions. Saussure adds, "Signs function, then, not through their intrinsic value but through their relative position" (1915/1966:118). We can see this readily enough in language, but it also holds for texts of all kinds. Nothing has meaning in itself and every concept takes its meaning from a binary opposition. This applies to gender, which, from the Bible to this present day, was seen in binary or oppositional terms: Adam and Eve, male and female, man and woman. We read in the Bible:

> Then God said, "Let us make man in our image, after our likeness. And let them have dominion over the fish of the sea and over the birds of the heavens and over the livestock and over all the earth and over every creeping thing that creeps on the earth." So God created man in his own image, in the image of God he created him; male and female he created them.

From the beginning pages of the Bible, we learn that there are two genders—male and female, a binary opposition. But all through history, we have found that this binary opposition is too simplistic and does not account for the many variations in gender identity, now subsumed under the concept "non-binary."

This includes the now simplistic opposition straight / heterosexual and gay / homosexual.

Judith Butler

Judith Butler's *Gender Trouble: Feminism and the Subversion of Identity* is widely accepted as a seminal contribution to our understanding of gender. In her preface to a revised version of the book, she suggests that our notions of gender have changed and aren't as fixed as they used to be (1999: xxix):

> Precisely because "female" no longer appears to be a stable notion, its meaning is as troubled and unfixed as "woman," and because both terms gain their troubled significations only as relational terms, this inquiry takes as its focus gender and the relational analysis it suggests. Further, it is no longer clear that feminist theory ought to try to settle the questions of primary identity in order to get on with the task of politics.

She writes, in the first chapter of *Gender Trouble,* titled "Subjects of Sex / Gender / Desire," about the relationship that exists between sex and gender (1999:9,10):

> Originally intended to dispute the biology-is-destiny formulation, the distinction between sex and gender serves the argument that whatever biological intractability sex appears to have, gender is culturally constructed: hence, gender is neither the casual result of sex nor as seemingly fixed as sex....If gender is the cultural meanings that the sexed body assumes, then gender cannot be said to follow from a sex in any one way. Taken to its logical limit, the sex/gender distinction suggests a radical discontinuity between sexed bodies and culturally constructed genders.

This means that for Butler, gender is not "fixed" but is socially constructed, which suggests that one can change one's gender since it does not automatically follow from one's sex "in any way."

LGBTIQ+ and Culture

In recent years, where lesbians, gays, bisexuals, transsexuals, intersexuals, and genderqueer people have come out of their closets to play an important role in our discourse about sex and gender. They also now play an important role in our politics, entertainment, and other aspects of life. Gender Agenda, a website, offers the following description of members of the LGBTIQ+ world:

> LGBTIQ+ is an inclusive acronym encompassing all minority sexual and gender identities, as well as atypical biological sex or Intersex. Trans* is inclusive of all transgender persons from transsexuals to transvestites,

> some of whom may identify as binary male or female, irrespective of biological/body sex and others as outside the binary of just two genders. Q+ includes all other identities including Asexual, Pansexual, Genderqueer, Non-binary, Questioning, etc. People whose gender is non-conforming may also identify as an LGB or another minority sexual identity, or they may identify as heterosexual. No disrespect or erasure is intended in not using one of the longer LGBTIQ2SA type initialisms or terms appropriate to different languages and cultures. There is no international agreement on how to extend LGBT to be more inclusive of all Gender and Sexual Diversities.
>
> http://www.genderagenda.net/LGBTIQdefinition.htm

If gender is a performance and because there are now many variations in gender identity that are available to people, we can consider people's identities in a new, more understanding, and more humane way.

Chapter 10

The Insurrection on January 6 and the Trial of Donald Trump

When a mob of people, sent by Donald Trump, invaded the Capitol, it was the worst thing that had happened to the Capitol since the British burned it down in 1814. On Dec. 7, 1941, a "day that will live in infamy," as President Franklin Delano Roosevelt put it, Japanese bombers attacked Pearl Harbor in a stealth attack, with calamitous results. On December 11, 2001, Islamic terrorists flew two huge airplanes into the twin towers in New York City, leading to the destruction of the skyscrapers and the deaths of more than 3,000 people. On that day, Americans suddenly learned that their oceans would no longer protect them.

Figure 10.1: The Insurrection at the Capitol Building.

Photo by the Author from Television.

An Attack on the Capitol by Americans

Both of these attacks were from foreign adversaries. What was remarkable about the attack on the Capitol on January 6, 2021, was that it was done by Americans—by an American mob summoned to Washington D.C. by the president on that date and sent by him to disrupt the proceedings at the Capitol in a desperate attempt by Trump to maintain power. Originally, the gathering was planned for late in January but Trump changed the date to January 6 and to a time when the members of Congress were certifying the election. Trump brought the people to Washington at the precise time when he could send them to attack the Capitol and prevent the certification of Joe Biden as president.

It is difficult to estimate how many people were in that mob but it is reasonable to suggest many hundreds. What was remarkable was the fury of the mob, a collection of neo-fascists, white supremacists, anti-Semites, Q-Anon followers, and others who ransacked the Capitol, smeared feces on the walls in places, broke windows, trashed the offices of Nancy Pelosi, killed one person and injured more than one hundred.

Fortunately, the mob couldn't find Vice President Pence, who they wanted to hang, Nancy Pelosi who they wanted to kill, or other members of the House of Representatives or the Senate. There could have been mass killings had the mob found anyone from Congress. The members of the mob were motivated by many different things, such as a feeling of being left out, a sense that "elites" on the two coasts looked down on them, by racism, and countless other things. Many of them, it turns out, were in debt and all of them, it seems, were very angry—mirroring Trump's anger.

The most significant motivation was "the Big Lie," which is Trump's false claim that he really won the election and that it was stolen from the people. This was reflected in the chants made by the mob, "stop the steal." Trump repeated this lie many times over the months before the election and a large number of people, mostly Republicans, still actually believe that the election was stolen from Trump. This, despite numerous reports about the election being fair and honest and countless lawsuits by Trump that were thrown out of court.

Many people in the mob thought they were being "patriots" and many said that since they were sent to the Capitol by the president, they were not doing anything illegal. Now that many of these so-called "patriots" are being investigated by the FBI and other governmental agencies, some of their lawyers are arguing that the members of the mob they are representing were "duped" by Trump. While the mob was attacking the Capitol, Trump watched them from the White House, was pleased with what they were doing, members of the White House staff reported, and did nothing to stop them for a long time.

The attack was Trump's last chance, he thought, to keep power. He believed, falsely, that Vice President Pence could refuse to accept the certification and allow Trump to overthrow the result of the election and remain as president. When Pence refused to do so, Trump turned the crowd on Pence, which explains why so many of them were screaming "Hang Pence."

Trump was willing to throw Pence, who had been faithful to Trump for four years, "under the bus," without a second thought when Pence explained that he didn't have the power to annul the election since his role was merely ceremonial.

Figure 10.2: The Trial of Donald J. Trump.

Photo from Television by the Author.

Trump was impeached a second time and then brought to trial by the Senate for a second time. The second trial was much different from the first trial since the events involved in the second trial, the storming of the Capitol, was shown on television as it happened and everyone was familiar with it.

The U. S. Senate Trial of Donald J. Trump

In this trial, run by a team of members of the Democratic Party in the House of Representatives, the presentations were backed up with the use of many videos and images. The Democrats recognized how powerful images are and started the trial with a thirteen-minute video showing the attack and used videos of Trump's speech on January 6th and many other videos to make their points.

For example, they showed Trump making his speech to the mob that he had assembled, in which he repeated the "Big Lie" about his having won the election, by a landslide, and, as the Democrats showed, sent the members of the mob to the Capitol, telling them to "fight like hell or you won't have a country anymore." They also showed many of his tweets and videos in which he said "We love you, you're very special." He also told them to "remember this day," casting the mob violence as something of which they should be proud.

An article by Todd Frankel in a *Washington Post* email on Feb. 10, 2021, with the title, "A majority of the people arrested for Capitol insurrection had a history of financial trouble" helps explain, in part, what motivated the mob that attacked the Capitol. They were motivated, it was found, by financial insecurity and grievances:

> Nearly 60 percent of the people facing charges related to the Capitol insurrection showed signs of prior money troubles, including bankruptcies, notices of eviction or foreclosure, bad debts, or unpaid taxes over the past two decades, according to a Washington Post analysis of public records.

The group's bankruptcy rate — 18 percent — was nearly twice as high as that of the American public, The Post found. A quarter of them had been sued for money owed to a creditor. And 1 in 5 of them faced losing their home at one point, according to court filings. The financial problems are revealing because they offer potential clues for understanding why so many Trump supporters — many with professional careers and few with violent criminal histories — were willing to participate in an attack egged on by the president's rhetoric painting him and his supporters as undeserving victims.

We must keep in mind that the Capitol is a sacred space in America and the violation of the Capitol by the mob was especially traumatic since the Capitol building is connected to so much American history. Many journalists and academics suggested that the case made by the Democrats against Trump and the insurrectioners was very effective, but they also recognized that it was unlikely that there would be seventeen Republicans siding with the Democrats to convict Trump. This was because the Republican senators feared being primaried and losing their seats in the Senate. And with that loss, all the privileges, the sense of power, and the high status that comes with being a senator. Because of Trump's hold over his base, he had turned the Republicans in the Senate into a herd of sheep.

Elite Impunity

In the February 12, 2021 issue of Daily 202 (from *The Washington Post*), written by Olivier Knox, we read: "Trump said the system is 'rigged.' Democrats say his acquittal will prove it." The article explains:

> The managers spent hours quoting the selfie-taking seditionists claiming to be under orders from Trump, often in videos taken by the insurrectioners themselves. Those arrested and charged could face years, or even decades, in prison. Trump, if convicted, could face at most a new stain on his legacy.
>
> https://www.washingtonpost.com/politics/2021/02/12/daily-202-trump-said-system-is-rigged-democrats-say-his-acquittal-will-prove-it/

Trump's speech before the insurrection had no overt calls for his supporters to enter the Capitol or resort to violent means. But it included plenty of allusions to the idea that Congress accepting Biden's victory was a result that must be stopped.

Nicholas Fandos of *The New York Times* wrote an important article on page one of the February 11, 2021 edition with the title, "Democrats Trace Trump Mob's Path in Chilling Detail" that starts with the House impeachment managers opening:

> ….their prosecution of Donald J. Trump with a point-by-point account of the former president's monthlong campaign to overturn his election loss and goad his supporters to join him, bringing its most violent spasms to life with never-before-seen security footage from inside the Capitol of the Jan. 6 assault he is charged with inciting.

Because the arguments of the Democrats fell on deaf ears, Trump's lawyers made a relatively brief argument, suggesting he was protected by the first amendment. They didn't need to make a solid defense since they knew what the outcome would be when they started. Even though the U.S. Senate didn't convict Trump, the case made by the Democrats had a second purpose: to educate the American public about the events leading up to the insurrection and to show, in some detail, the role that Trump played in bringing the mob together and setting off the insurrection. There can be little doubt that for most of the American public, Trump's behavior was seen as reprehensible, and his image, and that of the Republican Party, had been greatly diminished.

Chapter 11

Haredi:

Strictly Orthodox Jews

There are an estimated million and a half Haredi or strictly Orthodox Jews in the world, who are all easily recognized by the clothes they wear and their side curls.

Figure 11.1: Haredi in Their Typical Dress.

Photo by the Author from Television.

The Haredi

An article by Raysh Weiss, "Haredim (Charedim) or Ultra-Orthodox Jews" discusses the Haredi as follows:

> Haredi are perhaps the most visibly identifiable subset of Jews today. They are easy to spot–Haredi men in black suits and wide-brimmed black hats, Haredi women in long skirts, thick stockings, and headcoverings–but much harder to understand. Indeed, the history, beliefs, and practices of these devout Jews remain a mystery to many who live outside their cloistered communities. The word "Haredi" is a catchall term, either an adjective or a noun, which covers a broad array of theologically, politically, and socially conservative Orthodox Jews, sometimes referred to as "ultra-Orthodox." What unites haredim is their absolute reverence for Torah, including both the Written and Oral Law, as the central and determining factor in all aspects of life. Consequently,

> respect and status are often accorded in proportion to the greatness of one's scholarship, and leadership is linked to learnedness.
>
> In order to prevent outside influence and contamination of values and practices, haredim strive to limit their contact with the outside world, avoiding, as much as possible, both non-haredi Jews and non-Jews. Interaction with outsiders is generally confined to basic economic contact and unavoidable public interactions, such as going to the post office. However, certain groups of haredim, notably, but not exclusively, members of Chabad Lubavitch, do make contact with non-Haredi Jews for the purpose of *Kirov*–encouraging others to adopt a more stringent religious observant behavior.
>
> https://www.myjewishlearning.com/article/haredim-charedim/

The Haredi are of interest to us because members of ultra-Orthodox or as they prefer, strictly Orthodox Jewish communities, have no problems with their identities. From the moment of birth until their death, they are members of a community that shapes their entire lives and which provides powerful support to their identities. Haredi men are easily recognizable by the fedoras and the dark suits they wear, and other garments signifying their beliefs.

Haredi and the Four Lifestyles

In an earlier chapter, I discussed the work of Mary Douglas and grid-group theory. I pointed out that according to Douglas, there are four "lifestyles" that are generated by two phenomena: weak or strong group boundaries and few or many rules and prescriptions. One of these four groups, elitists (sometimes called hierarchical elitists), is subject to numerous rules and prescriptions and strong group boundaries. This lifestyle, in its curious way, helps explain the Haredi.

Haredi live in a culture with very strong boundaries and countless rules of behavior (and avoidances) and tend to avoid interactions with the general public in order to help sustain their religious identities. In a sense, to the degree possible, Haredi live in closed communities where they both receive support from other members of the community and provide support to each other.

Wikipedia offers some insights into Haredi life:

> Haredi life, like Orthodox Jewish life in general, is very family-centered. Boys and girls attend separate schools, and proceed to higher Torah study, in a yeshiva or seminary, respectively, starting anywhere between the ages of 13 and 18. A significant proportion of young men remain in yeshiva until their marriage (which is usually arranged through facilitated dating). After marriage, many Haredi men continue their Torah studies in a kollel.

> Studying in secular institutions is often discouraged, although educational facilities for vocational training in a Haredi framework do exist. In the United States and Europe, the majority of Haredi males are active in the workforce. For various reasons, in Israel, around half of their members do not work, and most of those who do are not officially a part of the workforce. Haredi families (and Orthodox Jewish families in general) are usually much larger than non-Orthodox Jewish families, with as many as twelve or more children.[11] Haredi Jews are typically opposed to the viewing of television and films, and the reading of secular newspapers and books. There has been a strong campaign against the Internet, and Internet-enabled mobile phones without filters have also been banned by leading rabbis. In May 2012, 40,000 Haredim gathered at Citi Field, a baseball park in New York City, to discuss the dangers of unfiltered Internet. The event was organized by the Ichud HaKehillos LeTohar HaMachane. The Internet has been allowed for business purposes so long as filters are installed.
>
> https://en.wikipedia.org/wiki/Haredi_Judaism

The Haredi represent an important means of dealing with a significant problem Judaism faces: preventing Jews from assimilating and losing their Jewish identities. It can also be seen as a response to the Holocaust, in which six million Jews were murdered. In Israel, the Haredi have considerable political power and many survive because of bounties by the Israeli government since many of the Haredi men don't work but spend all their time studying the Torah.

Different Kinds of Haredi

It is important to recognize that there are several different kinds of Haredi, that they are not all alike. For example, one sect or court or whatever you want to call them, the Satmar Jews, differentiate themselves from other Haredi by the fur hats they wear. Many of the sects are named after the city where they originated.

Figure 11.2: Satmar Fur Shtreimel.

Photo by Author.

These hats can cost thousands of dollars since they often use expensive furs. So there are many varieties of Haredi or Ultra-Orthodox as most people call them (though they prefer the term strictly Orthodox) but they are all similar in terms of their lifestyles and their desire to live "A Life Apart," to quote the title of a CBS television show about another ultra-Orthodox group, Hasids. All of these ultra-Orthodox groups represent an attempt to save Judaism from the forces of assimilation that represent, ultra-Orthodox Jews believe, an existential threat to the survival of Judaism. Their solution is the separation into emotionally binding communities that provide support to the religious identities of their adherents but at a considerable cost. These ultra-Orthodox communities are usually led by a very senior and often very old rabbi, "the Rebbe," and resemble, in some ways, cults.

Judaism as a Civilization

Mordecai M. Kaplan, in his book *Judaism as a Civilization: Toward a Reconstruction of American-Jewish Life,* provides a different solution to the problem of assimilation. He writes (2010:178):

> Apart from the life which, as a citizen, the Jew shares with the non-Jews, his life should consist of certain social relationships to maintain, cultural interests to foster, activities to engage in, organizations to belong to, amenities to conform to, moral and social standards to live up to as a Jew. All this constitutes the element of otherness. *Judaism as otherness is thus something for more comprehensive than Jewish religion. It includes the nexus of a history, literature, language, social organization, folk sanctions, standards of conduct, social and spiritual ideals, esthetic values, which in their totality form a civilization.* It is not only Judaism, the religion, that is threatened but Judaism, the civilization. What endangers that civilization is not only the preoccupations with the civilizations of other peoples but also the irrelevance, remoteness and vacuity of Jewish life.

Kaplan spends almost 600 pages providing his critique of traditional forms of Judaism in America and offering his theory that Judaism will survive only when it recognizes that it is a distinctive and beneficent kind of civilization. What Kaplan wants is a way of integrating Judaism into contemporary life by recognizing, he argues that it is not just a religion but a civilization. He is thus at an opposite pole from the ultra-Orthodox Jews who fear that connection with the contemporary world will lead to a horrific contamination and so they choose to live a life apart. It is difficult to know, at this point in time, whose answer is best.

Chapter 12
Parodies:
Problems in Comedic Identity

> *Scintillate, scintillate, globule vivific*
> *Fain would I fathom thy nature specific.*
> *Loftily poised in ether capacious,*
> *Strongly resembling a gem carbonaceous.*
>
> Parody of "Twinkle, Twinkle, Little Star."

We can understand parody to involve a humorous imitation of a style of writing or speaking, imitation of a genre, or imitation of a particular text. For parody to "work" best, the reader must be familiar with what is being imitated or ridiculed.

Parody and Intertextuality

Technically speaking, parody is an example of intertextuality, described by Neil R. Norrick in his essay, "Intertextuality in Humor," as follows (1989:117-118):

> Intertextuality occurs any time one text suggests or requires reference to some other identifiable text or stretch of discourse, spoken or written. Scholarly writing seems to make its intertextual references as accurate and conspicuous as possible through documentation, while everyday conversation borrows freely from sources often left unnamed, and literature delights in disguise, obscure allusion, and parody.

The concept of intertextuality comes from the writing of the Russian theorist Mikhail Bakhtin, who writes in his classic work, *Rabelais and His World* (1984:84):

> Medieval parody, especially before the twelfth century, was not concerned with the negative, the imperfections of specific cults, ecclesiastical orders, or scholars which could be the object of derision and destruction. For the medieval parodist everything was without exception comic. Laughter was as universal as seriousness; it was directed at the whole world, at history, at all societies, at ideology.

What Bakhtin wrote about parody and its interest in ridiculing everything still applies to modern parodists, who revel in ridiculing the style of writers like Hemingway, genres such as soap operas, and texts such as *Star Wars* and James Bond movies. Wherever there is distinction and identity, parodists find their targets. There are, I suggest, three kinds of parodies:

1. Parodies of style, such as the way college bulletins are written.
2. Parodies of famous texts, such as parodies ridiculing James Bond spy stories.
3. Parodies of genres, such as spoofs of newspapers, soap operas, or romance novels.

Annie Gerin, a professor of art history at the University of Quebec in Montreal, offers another definition of parody in her book, *Devastation and Laughter: Satire, Power, and Culture in the Early Soviet State, 1920s-1930s* (2018:132):

> Parody is essentially transtexual, that is to say, it necessarily refers to another pre-extant work. A parody is a productive imitation created to comment on, mock, or trivialize its original source, often, but not always leading to satire. It resembles its referent, but also exhibits differences and thence plays with the expectations of the viewer, which it challenges to a certain degree. For parody, as a transtextual form, to be efficient, its source needs to be well known by the public. Because of this, it is often ambivalent, at once affirming the cultural importance of the source and mocking it or ridiculing practices that are contiguous to it.

There is, we see, a double-edged sword to parody: in one sense, it honors its source, but in truth, it actually is an attack on it, mocking and trivializing it. The pleasure we get from parody involves our appreciation of the way the parody attacks the "aura" of the distinctiveness of the source and plays with it, using various mechanisms of humor in doing so.

The Forty-Five Techniques of Humor

Table 12.1: 45 Techniques of Humor by Category.

LANGUAGE	LOGIC	IDENTITY	ACTION
Allusion	Absurdity	Before/After	Chase
Bombast	Accident	Burlesque	Slapstick
Definition	Analogy	Caricature	Speed
Exaggeration	Catalogue	Eccentricity	
Facetiousness	Coincidence	Embarrassment	
Insults	Comparison	Exposure	
Infantilism	Disappointment	Grotesque	
Irony	Ignorance	Imitation	
Misunderstanding	Mistakes	Impersonation	
Over literalness	Repetition	Mimicry	
Puns/Wordplay	Reversal	Parody	
Repartee	Rigidity	Scale	
Ridicule	Theme & Variation	Stereotype	
Sarcasm	Unmasking		
Satire			

Table by Author.

In my work on humor, I identified forty-five techniques that generate comedic results. I found these techniques by conducting a search of humorous texts in which I looked for the technique or techniques generating humor. When I collected my forty-five techniques, I discovered that they could be placed under four categories: humor involving language, logic, identity, and action. I placed parody under humor involving identity, along with other techniques of humor such as burlesque, caricature, impersonation, and imitation. I distinguish between imitation and parody, reserving the term parody for literary works of one kind or another.

Table 12.2: Techniques of Humor Numbered and in Alphabetical Order.

1. Absurdity	16. Embarrassment	31. Parody
2. Accident	17. Exaggeration	32. Puns
3. Allusion	18. Exposure	33. Repartee
4. Analogy	20. Grotesque	35. Reversal
6. Bombast	21. Ignorance	36. Ridicule
7. Burlesque	22. Imitation	37. Rigidity
8. Caricature	23. Impersonation	38. Sarcasm
9. Catalogue	24. Infantilism	39. Satire
10. Chase Scene	25. Insults	40. Scale, Size
11. Coincidence	26. Irony	41. Slapstick
12. Comparison	27. Literalness	42. Speed
13. Definition	28. Mimicry	43. Stereotypes
14. Disappointment	29. Mistakes	44. Theme & Variation.
15. Eccentricity	30. Misunderstanding	45. Unmasking

Table by Author.

I explain these techniques and offer examples of each in my books *An Anatomy of Humor* and *Blind Men and Elephants: Perspectives on Humor.* Now let me use these techniques to deconstruct a radio Erevan joke. These jokes ridicule the Russian government.

> A person calls Radio Erevan and asks, "Is it true that comrade Gorshinko won 5000 rubles at the lottery?" "Yes," replies Radio Erevan. "But it was not comrade Gorshinko but comrade Kataev, and it was not 5000 rubles but 10,000 rubles, and he didn't win it at the lottery but lost it gambling."

In this joke, we find the dominant technique is number 35, reversal. Radio Erevan says "yes" to the question but reverses every part of the event involving comrade Gorshinko. There is also 39, satire. These Radio Erevan jokes satirize Russian politics. One of the most famous of these Radio Erevan jokes goes as follows: "Would it be possible to bring Socialism to the Sahara?" "Yes," replies Radio Erevan, "But after the first five-year plan, we'll have to import sand."

An Example of a Parody of Style

Let me offer an example of parody of style—Woody Allen's parody of the kind of writing found in college bulletins, titled "Spring Bulletin," which appeared in his book, *Getting Even* (1978:42):

> Introduction to Psychology
>
> The theory of human behavior. Why some men are called "lovely individuals" and why there are others you just want to pinch. Is there a split between mind and body and, if so, which is better to have? Aggression and rebellion are discussed. (Students interested in these aspects of psychology are advised to take one of the Winter Term courses: Introduction to Hostility; Intermediate Hostility; Advanced Hatred; Theoretical Foundations of Loathing.) Special consideration is given to the study of consciousness as opposed to unconsciousness, with many helpful hints on how to remain conscious.

While this passage is humorous on its own, it draws its power from ridiculing the way courses are described in college bulletins. People who are not familiar with the way courses are described in college catalogs wouldn't appreciate or "get" Allen's humor, though they may find his description amusing. Parodies use many other techniques of humor: ridicule, exaggeration, absurdity and so on, to generate humor. In a sense, then, parody is a meta-technique that relies on other techniques found in my list of techniques. It is often the case that two or three techniques are found in a humorous text. Jokes, described as short texts meant to muse with punch lines, often have two or three techniques in them. Parodies of the style of Ernest Hemingway are very popular and parodies of texts such as *Star Wars* or of James Bond novels and films are also commonly made. It is important that a text that is parodied be distinctive in some manner and be well known.

A Parody of a Newspaper

In a book titled, *A Decade of Dark Humor: How Comedy, Irony, and Satire Shapes Post-9/11 America,* Jamie Warner has a chapter on "Humor, Terror, and Dissent: *The Onion after 9/11"* that discusses how *The Onion* functioned as an agent of satirical insurgency through its use of parody (2011:65):

> *The Onion* is a satirical parody of a newspaper. To achieve the double layer of meaning necessary for irony, *The Onion* must look like a newspaper and it does. It has sections entitled "Video," "Sports," and "World," as well as "Election 08," "Local," and "Nat'l" sections very similar to the online versions of *The New York Times* and *The Washington Post.* There are opinion columns, "American Voices," and "Horoscope"

> sections. The virtual format mirrors a "real" online paper: pictures punctuate the story lines with "serious" captions.
>
> But *The Onion* is not "real" news and this helps create the ambiguity in meaning necessary for irony. While *The Onion* looks like a real news source and relies on real-world events, it is replete with technical misrepresentations and false statements. Its stories, features, and columns are fake—lies in the strictest factual sense. They include quotations from imaginary people, imaginary quotations from real people, and make-believe scenarios, settings, and situations....Parodying the sober and seemingly impartial language and layout of a newspaper gives the content an air of legitimacy, objectivity, and respectability which then allows an automatic contrast with both the judgmental, yet mischievous and funny satirical content of many of the articles.

What we learn from this discussion is that parodies also often derive their humor from being ironic and satirical and maybe other techniques such as exaggeration and facetiousness. Parody is one of the most widely used techniques of humor because it enables people to compare the parody to the original text being parodied. This means a text only works as a parody if people can compare parody with what is being parodied. But parodies also work, even if people don't recognize a text as a parody, because parodies usually contain other techniques of humor that provide people with pleasure and generate mirthful laughter.

The Why Theories of Humor

My list of techniques differs from most theories of humor, which are what I describe as "why" theories that attempt to explain why we find something funny. My list is an attempt to explain what makes us laugh. There are a few "why" theories. One is from Freud and argues that humor is based on masked aggression. A second is from Aristotle and many other philosophers and thinkers and argues that humor is based on a sense of superiority.

Aristotle said that comedy is an "imitation of men who are worse than average," of people who are "ridiculous." Many other thinkers accept this theory. Probably the most widely accepted theory of humor argues that it is based on incongruity, on the difference between what we expect and what we get. As the philosopher Schopenhauer described it, quoted in Ralph Piddington's *The Psychology of Laughter* (1963:171):

> The cause of laughter in every case is simply the sudden perception of the incongruity between a concept and the real objects which have been thought through it in some relation, and laughter itself is just the expression of this incongruity.

The problem with these why theories is that they exist at a high level and don't explain how a parody, or any other example of humor, generates humor at a granular level. Humor is something that has interested and fascinated philosophers and scholars in many disciplines for thousands of years and there are countless books on the subject and every aspect of the subject that one can imagine. Parody, we see, is a technique of humor that can incorporate many other techniques and use them for comedic purposes, so parodists can also use satire, exaggeration, facetiousness, insults, and many other techniques to amuse readers.

Chapter 13

Ivy League and Elite Universities and Branding

Students applying to universities generally get acceptance notifications by the beginning of April, since they have to commit to attending a college by May 1st, as a rule. When I went to college in 1950, we got our acceptance notifications by letter and everyone knew what a thin letter meant—rejection, and a fat letter meant—acceptance.

Figure 13.1: Veritas Seal of Harvard University.

First Experience of Significant Failure

Not being accepted by an elite college or university is the first time many young people experience an important rejection and is often a traumatic experience. That is because, among other things, one's university plays a major role in shaping one's identity. The competition to attend elite universities is intense. In 2021 Harvard University had 57,000 applications and had an acceptance rate of five percent. Harvard College admits around 2000 students a year, which means that huge numbers of students who apply to Harvard are rejected.

The students who apply to Harvard College often apply to half a dozen or more other elite universities, such as other Ivy League schools such as Radcliffe or the Massachusetts Institute of Technology, the California Institute of Technology, and Stanford, all of which are selective. It is reasonable to suggest that most of the students who apply to the elite universities and others like them, are not accepted and some students, with very high-grade point averages and averages on whatever tests the universities require, don't get into many of them. I know of one student who got 1450 out of a possible 1500 on the most important entrance examination test he took and who was admitted to all of the elite universities to which he applied. He even turned down a thousand-dollar grant from Stanford so he could attend Harvard.

Universities and Branding

One reason students are so desperate to attend elite schools is that universities also brand the students who attend them, and that branding they can carry with them for the remainder of their lives. In an achieving society, such as the United States, getting into and graduating from an elite university offers one a sense of high status. I have several friends who graduated from Cornell, not the highest level school in the Ivy League, who have always found a way to mention the fact that they attended Cornell, forty or fifty years ago, in our conversations. At many schools, for one reason or another, a goodly number of freshman students transfer to other schools. Many freshmen find life at a university too demanding and not as much "fun" as they thought it would be. Being a freshman is stressful and full of anxiety and many students bring to their universities all kinds of psychological problems that they were able to contain and control while living at home. The transfer rate at elite universities is minimal. Having been fortunate enough to get into an elite school, students are reluctant to leave and discard the prestige they obtained by being admitted. Attending an elite university also brings students into contact with other students with similar intellectual abilities and students make connections that often last them for decades.

Students at elite universities also tend to socialize with members of the opposite sex (or the same sex) from other elite universities and tend to marry people with the same high status. It is more likely that a student from Harvard will socialize with and marry a woman from a school like Radcliffe or Wellesley than Northeastern University or Boston University, both of which are in Boston. The newspaper articles about wealthy families who paid college entrance fixers hundreds of thousands of dollars to get their children into the University of Southern California and other universities is a testimonial to how important people think it is to go to a selective university and how desperate they were to get their children into the right school. A newspaper article I read discussed a couple who said their daughter wanted to go to USC so she could go to the football games and attend fraternity parties.

Other Universities

There are, of course, countless other colleges and universities where students obtain excellent educations. Some students aren't psychologically mature enough to compete with other students in highly selective schools but do well in small schools where they get more personal attention. And there are community colleges and state universities where students can get fine educations at a fraction of the cost of the elite schools. Most Americans are educated at state universities and non-selective schools, and manage quite well—even if they can't enjoy the pleasure of being branded a Harvard man, a Wellesley girl, or a graduate of other elite schools.

There is also the problem that students at elite universities face: have they peaked at seventeen or eighteen when they are admitted to an elite university? As one graduate of Harvard told me, shortly after graduating, "It's all downhill from now on." Maybe, for millions of young students, it is better to have no place to go but up rather than no place to go but down!

Chapter 14

Tattoos and Dramatized Self

People have been getting tattooed for thousands of years for a variety of reasons. As Marcel Danesi explains in his book, *Concise Dictionary of Popular Culture* (2017:254):

> TATTOO
>
> Body decoration that dates back as far as 8000 BCE. In the ancient world, it was associated with authority figures. In Egypt, for example, it was reserved for the nobility. The ancient Greeks and Romans, however, used tattoos to identify slaves and criminals. Tattoos became symbolic of early motorcycle gangs, which remains so to this day. The adoption of tattooing as a pop culture trend began with metal culture in the early 1970s, since band members displayed their tattoos prominently in their performances. The **Rolling Stones** made tattoos a **fad** with their popular 1981 **album** *Tattoo You.* Today, tattooing has evolved into a society-wide trend, having lost most, if not all, of its previous symbolic associations. Tattooing and the human stories behind it became a subgenre of specialty **channels,** such as TLC in the 2000s, with reality shows such as *Miami Ink,* which premiered in 2005 ending in 2008, and several spin-offs, including *LA Ink* and *NY Ink.*

We see from Danesi's discussion that tattoos have played important roles in ancient cultures and still play a role in contemporary ones, where many people become tattooed. For many people, tattoos are still negative signifiers of criminality and lower-class status so although tattoos are now popular, they still retain their transgressive origins.

Figure 14.1: Advertisement for Inkholics Tattoo Company.

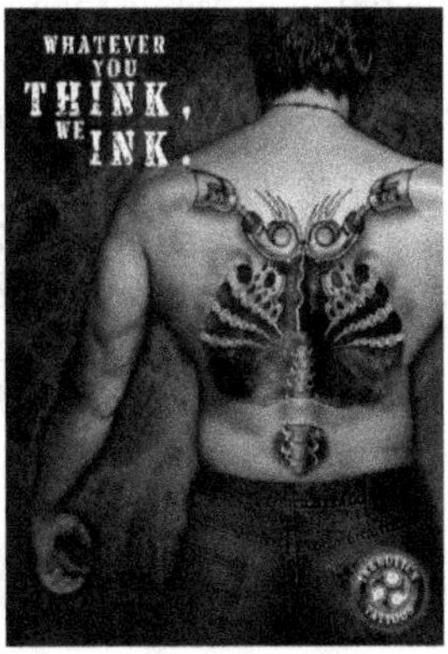

This advertisement emphasizes the creative aspects of tattoos and informs people that Inkholics can "ink" whatever anyone can "think" or want as far as the design of tattoos is concerned. The muscular body of the person tattooed suggests manliness and power.

Defining Tattoos

Wikipedia defines tattoos as follows:

> A tattoo is a form of body modification where a design is made by inserting ink, dyes and pigments, either indelible or temporary, into the dermis layer of the skin to change the pigment. The art of making tattoos is tattooing. Tattoos fall into three broad categories: purely decorative (with no specific meaning); symbolic (with a specific meaning pertinent to the wearer); and pictorial.
>
> https://en.wikipedia.org/wiki/Tattoo

We can see from this definition that there are different kinds of tattoos and they have several different functions, from being seen as a form of body beautification to announcing membership in a group of some kind. Danesi sees tattooing as a transgressive act, not being concerned with the boundaries of decorum and decency that have lost their original meaning and are now widely accepted. Since people have been getting tattoos for thousands of years, we may suggest that they have important meanings for the people who get the tattoos. Some tattoos are simple designs, some tattoos are names of loved ones, some indicate gang membership, and some are pictures the people getting the tattoos think enhance their self-image.

Tattoos and the Psyche

We also have to consider the difference between the conscious meanings of a tattoo and the unconscious significance of the tattoo. It is reasonable to suggest that people who get tattoos are unaware of the hidden imperatives in their psyches that lead them to be tattooed. While the manifest function of a tattoo may be that they are a form of body adornment or decoration, their latent function may be an unconscious form of masochism, since they are a kind of body piercing and getting a tattoo is painful.

We can distinguish between the personal and social functions of tattoos. On the personal level, they are a form of decoration and, for many, a signifier of individuation and escape from parental and social control. On the social level, tattoos function as indications of a connection with others, countering the alienation many people feel while living in contemporary societies and, at the same time, signifiers of anomic or normless behavior. Tattoos, I believe, are a way of "dramatizing" the self, of calling attention to oneself and, in some cases, one's connection to groups, some of which border on criminality and some of which are criminal.

Atte Oksanen and Jussi Turtainen discuss the relation between the self and tattooing in their article, "A Life Told in Ink: Tattoo narratives and the Problem of the Self in Late Modern Society," which appeared in *Contexts*, Winter, 2004:

> Susan A. Phillips...argues that social class defines how tattoos are perceived. While middle-class tattooing seems to be a partly safe way of expressing the self, a lower-class status can change how other people read the signs of the body; the self-expressive status of tattooing as art can turn out to be the mark of criminality. The risk to be misinterpreted is at least virtual for the middle-class subjects.... On the one hand, it can perhaps be even an enjoyable form of voluntary and rather harmless risk-taking. On the other, it can turn out to be repressing for the self which might end in having to cover up the body. At least in some respects, a businessman who is wearing his 'full body suit' under his suit resembles a prisoner who tries to tattoo himself in secrecy.
>
> https://www.researchgate.net/publication/216530484_A_Life_Told_in_Ink_Tattoo_Narratives_and_the_Problem_of_the_Self_in_Late_Modern_Society

We can see that tattoos evoke all kinds of responses in people and have many meanings for the people who get tattoos—from escape from parental and social control and an expression of individualism and identity to signifiers of low social status and, in some cases, criminality.

Why People Get Tattoos

People who get tattoos may do so because they are looking for attention, and tattoos function as a means of "ego screaming," that is, a search for attention, and also as a signifier of defiance and rebellion. It has been estimated that about fifteen percent of adults in the United States have tattoos and around twenty-eight percent of adults younger than twenty-five. In an article, "Why Do People Get Tattoos," Milliann Kang and Katherine Jones offer the following insights into the phenomenon:

> Most tattooed people see their tattoos as unique aspects of themselves, but sociologists who study tattooing focus on group patterns and overall trends. They examine the influence of media and consumer culture and the influence of gender, sexuality, race, and class on "body politics." While no single explanation accounts for the increasing popularity of tattoos, researchers find that people use tattoos to express who they are, what they have lived through, and how they see themselves in relation to others and to their social worlds. Studies also find that people cannot fully control the meaning of their own tattooed bodies; the social

contexts in which they live shape the responses to and interpretations of their tattoos by others.

https://journals.sagepub.com/doi/10.1525/ctx.2007.6.1.42

What this passage reveals is that tattoos have a kind of double valence: people get tattoos to express aspects of themselves, as they see things, but people with tattoos cannot control the way others see the tattoos and feel about the people with the tattoos. Their article also calls our attention to the role of popular culture and the media on tattooing which has been called "body politics."

Becoming tattooed is a very complicated matter and has both individual, social, and in some cases, even political, significance. In articles I've read on the subject, many people who got tattoos said that their tattoos helped them deal with psychological problems, such as their hatred of their bodies and feelings of alienation and inadequacy. How people react to tattoos, we see, has a sociological dimension in that older middle-class and upper-class people tend to see tattoos as signifiers of lower-class status and perhaps even criminality. But their children do not feel the same way and often get tattoos, so tattoos are unreliable signifiers of social and economic class.

Chapter 15

Porsches and German Engineering

"German Engineering" is a marketing meme that German companies use to sell their products. The meme is based on a stereotype that people have, based in part on advertising, about the quality of German products—and most especially, as far as consumer culture is concerned, about automobiles.

Stereotypes

A stereotype is a commonly held belief about people based on their race, religion, ethnicity, gender, and similar matters. Stereotypes can be negative, positive, or neutral. Stereotypes are used in popular culture narratives because they provide a quick motivation to explain the behavior of characters. Many people are unaware of the stereotypes they hold but their behavior is affected by these stereotypes. And many stereotypes are negative.

Here are some popular jokes based on stereotyping:

> Heaven is where the cooks are French, the police are British, the mechanics are German, the lovers are Italian and everything is organized by the Swiss. Hell is where the cooks are British, the police are German, the mechanics are French, the lovers are Swiss, and everything is organized by the Italians.
>
> A ship sinks and the survivors find themselves stranded on a desert island. The Americans go into business. The French start nightclubs. The Germans build armament plants. After a year, the Americans ask the French, "Who are those people standing around there?" The French reply, "They're English…and still waiting to be introduced."
>
> UNESCO invites representatives of different countries to a conference on elephants. The following papers are given. The Englishman gives his paper on "Elephant Hunting in Colonial India." The Russian paper is titled "The Superiority of the Russian Elephant." The Italian reads "Elephants and the Renaissance." The Frenchman offers "The Love Life of the Elephant." The German offers "A Short Introduction in Ten Volumes to the Stud of the Elephant." The American reads "How to Raise Bigger and Better Elephants." An Israeli offers "Elephants and the Jewish Question." A Nigerian reads "Elephants and Racism." The Czechs offer "Why the Soviet Elephant is Our Idol."

Stereotyping jokes focus upon alleged or popularly held characteristics of nations and preoccupations members of those nations have about various topics. In the first joke, which is a classic, when you are in heaven, you will have a German mechanic, working it may be assumed, on a German automobile. In the other joke, a German propensity for doing things well is ridiculed.

Figure 15.1: Advertisement for Porsche 911 Turbo.

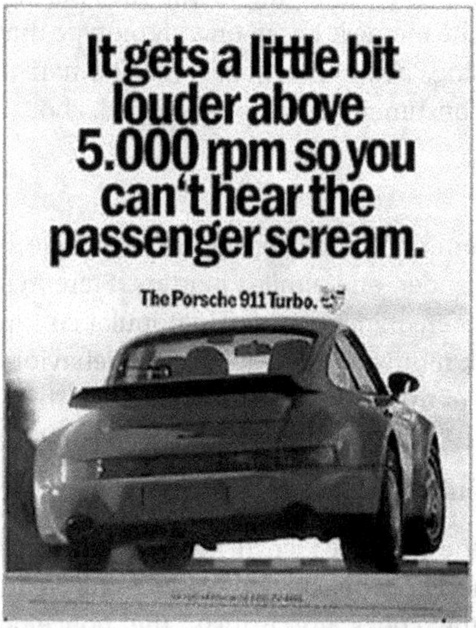

This advertisement focuses upon the power of the Porsche 911Turbo and has a comedic aspect to it, poking fun at the car's ability to make passengers scream—with delight, we can assume. The car costs around $200,000 and up.

Porsches and German Engineering

On the website of the Porsche Club of America we read:

> I don't want to perpetuate the stereotype, but there is something about the minutiae of German design that I find fascinating. Take the glove box in my Porsche Cayman, for instance. It had three distinct features I've never seen in another car. First was a set of clips to hold most any writing instrument, a clever pair of slots to accept, store, and eject my second and third most favorite CDs, and finally retractable cup-holder arms that swung out and retreated back into the housing with a click. It must have taken months to perfect this assembly, one iteration after another — meticulously tested, vetted, and re-engineered until flawless.
>
> Cars, in general, have never been manufactured as well as they are today. Therefore, setting yourself apart from other companies is incredibly

> challenging. Even brands once synonymous with chintzy, have improved to the point of consideration by even the most discernible buyers. But the phrase German Engineering isn't purely about exceptional design details. It is perfecting the ordinary, simplifying the impossible and the creation of brilliant products using the finest available materials. It is the very definition of the whole being greater than the sum of its parts.
>
> https://www.pca.org/news/2016-01-05/what-it-about-german-engineering

As we might expect, since this material appeared on a site of a club of Porsche enthusiasts, it is extremely positive. Porsche automobiles have a cult status in the United States and other countries as well.

The Porsche as a Cult Car

Porsche is a German brand of automobile that has maintained very high quality over the years. It competes with other German brands such as Audi, BMW, and Mercedes. Porsche has a cult following. An article in the July 2, 2020, *Wall Street Journal* (B6) titled, "All Your Inner Mario Andretti Could Desire," written by Lawrence Ulrich, describes, in rhapsodical prose, the Porsche 911 Turbo S, an automobile that costs more than $200,000. Ulrich offers some interesting statistics about Porsche:

> Porsche's record 256,000 global sales last year remain a blip in the VW Group's 10.8 million total. Yet the brand earned a staggering $4.75 billion operating profit, an average of about $18,500 per car, for a 16.6 percent net profit that tops every mass-market automaker.

He adds that more than 70 percent of all Porsches ever built are still being driven, and more than a million 911s have been made since 1964.

What we learn from this article is that the Porsche brand is very valuable, being an exemplar of German engineering and that sports cars, in general, are very profitable. The least expensive Porsche is the Macan, a sports utility automobile that costs $52,000 in the United States and is twice as expensive as compact SUV models such as the Honda CRV at $26,000 and the Toyota RAV4 at $27,000. The Macan is the best-selling model in the United States.

The average price of a new car sold in the United States is around $30,000 to $40,000 so Porches are beyond the reach, and maybe the desire, of most Americans. But at $60,000 for a car, Porsche is well within the range of people who purchase luxury cars.

Because many people who purchase new American automobiles add features to them that raise their price considerably, a $52,000 Porsche isn't as expensive as it might seem. And for that $52,000 you are getting German engineering.

Is German Engineering a Myth?

Ulrich's statistics on the longevity of Porsches attest to their quality but do other competing German automobiles such as Mercedes, Audi, and BMW have the same quality? It is difficult to say. *Consumer Reports* rates automobiles and consistently gives low ratings to some Mercedes models, suggesting they may be over-engineered and have control systems that are too complicated. Nevertheless, Mercedes is a popular brand and many people purchase them because they are seen as examples of German engineering. Having that Mercedes three-point star is a signifier, in the minds of those who purchase these cars, of status and sophistication.

An article on Autobytel's website offers information on the popularity of German automobiles in the United States:

> German cars are renowned for their leading-edge engineering. Mercedes-Benz, BMW, Audi, and Volkswagen have been responsible for the popularization of a wide variety of technical innovations like fuel injection, antilock brakes, electronic stability programs, front-wheel drive, all-wheel drive, and four-wheel independent suspension.
> At the same time, being on the leading edge of technology means German cars are often equipped with new systems that might well experience initial growing pains. There is no doubt the German-brand cars are well-built, no matter if that building takes place in Germany, Mexico, or the United States. But because of all they bring to the table in terms of tech and equipment, there are times when reliability can be challenging.
>
> https://www.autobytel.com/car-buying-guides/features/10-most-reliable-german-cars-132423/

In 2020, according to the Internet, the sales of German luxury automobiles wee (in thousands):

Audi	186
BMW	278
Mercedes	274
Porsche	57

Since Americans purchased more than 14 million automobiles and trucks in 2020, we can see that German Engineering plays a relatively small role in the total market for automobiles but it plays a major role in the market for luxury cars. *Consumer Reports* had an article on the "most popular" brands of cars" in America (2/16/2021) and Porsche cars came in seventh, ahead of other German luxury cars, but not by very much. The most popular brand of car was Tesla with a score of 84. The least popular was the Infiniti with a score of 48.

Porsche

Rating: 74 (out of a possible 100)

Number of models: 3

Owner Satisfaction Scores

DRIVING	COMFORT	INCAR ELECTRONICS	CABIN STORAGE	VALUE
5 / 5	5 / 5	2 / 5	1 / 5	1 / 5

Now, Porsche must compete with Japanese cars, Korean cars, luxury cars from other countries, and electric cars such as Tesla. The German automobile companies are now turning their attention to electric cars and soon it will be possible for people to enjoy the pleasures of German engineering in electric cars but not as much pleasure—no surprise to anyone interested in automobiles—as people who purchase Teslas.

Chapter 16

The GOP: Grand Old Party

A Problem with Political Identity

Figure 16.1: ErosGOPanalia or The Berger Hypottythesis.

Drawing by the author.

The drawing above was done to support a comedic article I wrote in which I suggested that members of the Republican party are anal erotics and that it is their toilet training that turns them into Republicans and supports their views about not spending money on government programs. As a joke, I sent a short article with this thesis to an economics journal and received a letter from the editor saying it was "unsuitable for publication in his journal or any that he could conceive of." I found that comment very satisfying.

The old "country club" Republican Party has been replaced by a much more extremist party whose members are now radical and reactionary. Some scholars have suggested it is no longer really a party but a political cult. The insurrectionists who attacked the Capitol, if they all weren't Republicans, were motivated by a Republican president, though many would argue that Trump isn't really a Republican but just someone who used the party for his own ends. It is generally understood that he ran for president as a publicity stunt and was surprised that he won.

Why is Anyone a Republican?

The question that bothers many people is this: why is anyone a Republican? For Democrats, the Republican Party is seen as anti-science, anti-rational, anti-immigrant, and little more than a conspiracy of people supporting politicians who seem only to want power and the prestige of holding political office. It has become, as a result of gerrymandering and its use of social and cultural wedge issues, an extremist political party, similar in many respects to some extreme right-wing parties found in Europe. Republicans are for guns and are anti-immigrant and anti-abortion. Their anti-abortion stance explains why evangelical Christians vote for them. Republicans love wedge issues.

Critics of the GOP (Grand Old Party) argue that it is led by careerists who have used wedge issues to win elections and has won the presidency many times, even though it lost the popular vote, because of inequities in our political system where states with just a few million people have the same number of senators as states like California, with forty million people. The Electoral College is also anti-democratic in that it has enabled candidates with fewer voters than their opponents to win the presidency.

So a minority party has controlled American politics for many years—even when there was a Democratic president. Until recently, Mitch McConnell, the "Grim Reaper," had been able to prevent the Democrats from getting anything done and has been able to populate the judiciary with conservative judges. And he helped Trump place three conservative judges on the Supreme Court.

In many Republican districts, who will win an election is not a problem but the primaries are. It is because of this situation that Trump has been able to dominate the Republicans in the House of Representatives and the Senate since he can influence the primaries. All the Republican politicians were afraid of Trump and his loyal base and many still are, even though Trump lost his bid for a second term as president. He will not admit it and has perpetrated a lie (what Democrats call "The Big Lie") about the matter, with catastrophic results for national unity and our democratic institutions.

Government is the Problem

The keyword to understand Republican political theory is freedom. Republicans like to talk about freedom all the time, such as the freedom to carry guns everywhere. Yet, they stand for preventing women from having a free choice if they want to have an abortion. Republicans believe it would seem, in freedom from governmental control of anything and freedom for individuals and corporations to do everything they want to do. As Ronald Reagan, one of the Republican saints, once explained, "Government is the problem."

Democrats, on the other hand, are the party of equality and believe in using government to solve problems. For Republicans, this is seen as socialism and a "big" government is considered a danger to their beloved freedom. What has happened is that thanks to Republican control of Congress, over the past decades, there has been a massive transfer of wealth from the poor and the middle classes to the upper classes. An example of this is the tax program passed by Trump and the Republicans whose benefits went mostly to wealthy people and corporations. And not anything to speak of, to Trump's beloved "base."

The Enigma of the 2020 Election

One thing that continues to puzzle many people is how so many members of the Republican Party can believe that Trump won the 2020 presidential election just because he claims he did.

A *U.S. News Report* suggests that around half of all Republicans believe Trump won the 2020 election and that it was stolen from him due to voter fraud:

> A new Reuters/Ipsos opinion poll found that 52% of Republicans believe that Trump won the election, compared to just 29% who believe Biden won, and more than two-thirds of Republicans, 68%, were concerned about "rigged" vote counting.
>
> https://www.usnews.com/news/politics/articles/2020-11-18/half-of-republicans-believe-president-trump-won-election-poll-finds

This statistic continues to amaze me, though the belief systems of people always are often hard to fathom. Many people believe that America has been visited by extra-terrestrials. Think, also, of all the Republicans (and some Democrats) who believe in QAnon which Wikipedia describes as follows:

> QAnon is a disproven and discredited far-right conspiracy theory alleging that a cabal of Satan-worshipping cannibalistic pedophiles is running a global child sex-trafficking ring and plotting against former U.S. President Donald Trump, who is fighting the cabal.
>
> https://en.wikipedia.org/wiki/QAnon

How ironic, as I suggested earlier in the book, that many Republicans say "Trump tells it like it is," when, according to *The Washington Post,* he told more than 30,000 lies in his speeches and tweets. There is reason to suggest that many Republicans have been brainwashed by Trump and his enablers in the Republican Party and refuse to accept reality. I would argue that the Republican Party is now a political cult, led by Donald Trump, the object of the Republican Party's affection.

Working-Class Authoritarianism

It may end up that Trump's base turns out to be a monkey on the backs of Republican politicians who think they are using the base but are, instead, being used by it. Political scientists have written about what they describe as "working-class authoritarianism" and it would seem that Trump's base and many other right-wing Republicans are working-class authoritarians. They see in him a reflection of their racism, anti-Semitism, anti-immigrant, authoritarian, and anti-democratic beliefs. There are some Republicans who are rebelling against the direction of the party and it is even conceivable that the party will eventually split into two very different parties: one moderate and the other ultra-conservative and close to being a fascist party. Some writers see Trump as the "friendly face of fascism" in the United States.

Chapter 17
The Politics of Identity and Identity Politics

Humans are political animals. In book 1 of his *Politics*, Aristotle writes:

> It is evident that the state is a creation of nature, and that **man is by nature a political animal**...that man is more of a political animal than bees or any other gregarious animals is evident. Nature, as we often say, makes nothing in vain, and man is the only animal whom she has endowed with the gift of speech...And it is a characteristic of man that he alone has any sense of good and evil, of just and unjust...and the association of living beings who have this sense makes a family and a state. [My boldface.]
>
> http://www.perseus.tufts.edu/hopper/text?doc=Perseus:abo:tlg,0086,035:1:1253a

Politics, which deals with relationships between people in every aspect of our lives, now seems to be the dominant aspect of people's identities in America, eclipsing religion, race, ethnicity, gender, and occupation.

The Politics of Identity

In the summer of 2021, as a result of the refusal of Donald Trump to admit defeat and because of his influence, many political scientists and students of American history and society believe that the "American democratic experiment" is in existential danger.

The political affiliations of Americans, as of 2021, are 49 percent Democrats (or leaning Democratic), 40 percent Republicans, and 11 percent Independents. Even though the Republicans are a minority party, six of the nine members of the Supreme Court were appointed by Republican presidents, fifty United States Senators are Republicans and they are close to being a majority in the United States House of Representatives. Twenty-seven states have Republican governors and their legislatures are controlled by Republicans.

Because the Republican Party is still controlled by the former president, Donald J. Trump, and because he refuses to admit that he lost the 2020 presidential election, many states run by Republicans, are now making changes in the way elections are run and counted and doing everything they can to make it more difficult for black people, people of color, and young people, who tend to vote Democratic, to vote. The Republicans say the bills they are passing in the states are to prevent fraud while the Democrats argue these bills are a means of suppressing votes for Democrats. Some scholars have suggested that Republicans now refuse to accept elections that they do not win as valid and are doing everything they can to make certain that they win all future elections.

It seems evident that former president Trump is authoritarian by nature and some writers have described him as a fascist. Recently it has come to light that he said something to the effect that "Hitler did some good things." Trump has many followers who are extremists, including neo-Nazis and white supremacists. And many who are in para-military organizations pose the most important threat to American democracy according to governmental agencies involved in national security. The attack on the Capitol Building on January 6, 2021, was the most serious attack on American democracy for more than a hundred years. It is generally understood that the attackers were spurred on by Trump.

Consider the following information found in a survey:

> A survey released Thursday by the conservative American Enterprise Institute (AEI) found that the vast majority of Republicans not only don't think Joe Biden was legitimately elected, nearly *40 percent* of them think political violence is justifiable and could be necessary. Those GOP respondents justifying violence said they agreed with the statement: "If elected leaders will not protect America, the people must do it themselves, even if it requires violent actions." Republicans gravitating towards violence while explicitly legitimizing it as a political tool is a dangerous precedent for the country. "I think any time you have a significant number of the public saying use of force can be justified in our political system, that's pretty scary," Daniel Cox, director of the AEI Survey Center on American Life, told NPR.
>
> https://slate.com/news-and-politics/2021/02/aei-poll-40-percent-republicans-conservatives-political-violence.html

It turns out that 53 percent of Republicans think that Trump won the presidential election, even though it is clear that this is not true. That is, they think that Joe Biden and the Democrats somehow stole the election from Donald Trump. That figure is much higher now, with around 80 percent of Republicans believing Trump won the election.

Because Trump politicized everything, wearing a mask became a political statement and many of Trump's supporters refused to wear masks, endangering themselves and others. We find the same thing with vaccinations, and now that there is a particularly dangerous version of the virus spreading, many Republicans who see getting vaccinated as another infringement on their liberty are dying, unnecessarily.

What we see from all this is that their political identity has become the dominant force in many people's lives and now, tragically, their deaths. Because of their political beliefs, millions of people are putting themselves and their loved ones at risk. America now is dividing into two groups: those who have been vaccinated and those who refuse to be vaccinated, with the second group now in mortal danger.

Identity Politics

When politics takes over everything, when members of families won't talk to one another because of their different political views (which started when Trump was president), when one's politics is central to one's identity, a society full of one-dimensional people like that is in serious trouble. This phenomenon is a new version of identity politics, which is traditionally associated with marginalized groups, as the Wikipedia article explains:

> Identity politics, as a mode of categorizing, are closely connected to the ascription that some social groups are oppressed (such as women, ethnic minorities, and sexual minorities); that is, the idea that individuals belonging to those groups are, by virtue of their identity, more vulnerable to forms of oppression such as cultural imperialism, violence, exploitation of labour, marginalization, or subjugation. Therefore, these lines of social difference can be seen as ways to gain empowerment or avenues through which to work towards a more equal society. In the United States, identity politics is usually ascribed to these oppressed minority groups who are fighting discrimination. In Canada and Spain, identity politics has been used to describe separatist movements; in Africa, Asia, and Eastern Europe, it has described violent nationalist and ethnic conflicts. Overall, in Europe, identity politics are exclusionary and based on the idea that the silent majority needs to be protected from globalization and immigration....During the 1980s, the politics of identity became very prominent and it was also linked to a new wave of social movement activism.
>
> https://en.wikipedia.org/wiki/Identity_politics

What we are experiencing now, in America, is a rebirth of identity politics, except that it is the politics of a political minority who are members of the Republican Party who feel that they are oppressed and are consumed, like Trump, by their countless grievances.

There is, in the United States, a crisis of legitimacy. Small states with just a few million people have two United States senators, which means that they are over-represented as far as political power is concerned. Wyoming, with 580,000 people, has the same number of senators as California, with almost forty million people. This means that small states with conservative populations have enormous power and have been able to prevent majorities from passing legislation that an overwhelming number of Americans want. The Senate has also been called the place where legislation (passed by Democrats in the House) goes to die.

An article, "American Needs to Break Up Its Biggest States," by Noah Millman, which appeared in the July 8, 2021 edition of *The New York Times* (A23) explains:

> The four largest states by population now make up roughly one-third of the population of the entire United States—more than the smallest 34 put together. This poses a critical problem for democratic legitimacy primarily because of the Senate. Those four states have only eight senators while the 34 smallest states have a supermajority of 68.

The Senate not only can block legislation but also approves many presidential appointments, members of the judiciary and treaties with other countries. In effect, due to the acute disproportion of representation, the Senate disenfranchises much of America's population. Consider also the Electoral College. In many recent presidential elections, the candidate who has gained the most votes has lost. The most recent case being the 2016 election in which Donald Trump received three million fewer votes than Hilary Clinton, yet won the election. It is difficult to know what will happen. As a result of the 2020 election, there is now a Democratic president, Joseph Biden, and the Democrats have a slim majority in the House of Representatives and fifty U.S. Senators, which gives them a majority since the Vice-President can cast a vote when there are ties. The population of the country is split with identity politics and political identities dominating governmental activities. Political life in American now has a dramatic quality and what is at stake is nothing less than the survival of the American democratic system as we have known it since the country was founded. In the 2022 election, if either party wins a few more House and Senate elections, the governance of the country will change in dramatic ways, especially since the Republican Party seems to be morphing into a political cult with many extremist, ultra-reactionary, and neo-fascistic members.

Benjamin Franklin said that "We have a republic if we can keep it." The question we face now in America is—can we keep it?

Chapter 18
The Seafarer's Self: Travel, Myth, and Identity

For many people, being a traveler or tourist is an important aspect of their personal identity. There is a certain cachet to being a traveler and having ventured to distant lands. Some travelers make all their travels on their own, but for large numbers of people, especially as they get older, taking a cruise is a form of soft travel that enables them to visit many interesting places in a relatively easy way. Once they get to the cruise ship. In some cases, that involves long-haul flights—such as from San Francisco to Dubai or New York to Bali.

Myth and Travel

In *Mythologies,* Roland Barthes ties travel on ships to the mythic—namely Noah's ark—and points our attention to an important element of travel, namely the desire of people from various social classes to maintain social distance from those not like themselves. Mircea Eliade, a scholar of religion who has written extensively on the subject of myths, describes myths as sacred histories and suggests in *The Sacred and The Profane* that they are "the paradigmatic model for all human activities" (1961:97,98). He also has written (1961:204,205) "The modern man who feels and claims that he is nonreligious still retains a large stock of camouflaged myths and degenerated rituals."

He offers as examples things like New Year's Eve parties, parties given when one is promoted, battles between monsters and heroes in films, and that kind of thing. I have developed what I call a "myth model" which argues that myth not only informs many of our daily activities but also plays a role in other matters, even if we might not recognize that this is the case or be aware of it as doing such. Let me suggest that we can also take a myth and find myths informing:

The Myth Model

A myth
The myth and psychoanalytic theory,
The myth and historical experience,
The myth reflected in elite literature,
The myth reflected in popular culture (and)
The myth as part of everyday life.

Let me offer an example of how myth pervades different aspects of travel in my "myth model" which deals with the mythological hero Odysseus—also known as Ulysses--as a paradigmatic figure, who can be seen as the UR traveler, the model for all travelers, even though most of us don't take such extended trips (many years) or encounter such danger (one after another). This discussion draws upon my analysis of myth in my book *Media, Myth and Society* (Palgrave Pivot, 2013) and other writings on tourism and travel over the years.

Figure 18.1: Mosaic of Odysseus chained to the ship's mast to prevent him from going to the Sirens.

Photo by the Author from the Bardo Museum in Tunisia.

The Myth Model and Travel/Tourism

The myth model always begins with a myth and then investigates, as I explained above, how that myth has informed various aspects of psychoanalytic theory, history, elite culture, popular culture, and everyday life. The myth chosen for this analysis of travel and tourism is the myth of Odysseus/Ulysses, which is found in Homer's classic book, *The Odyssey.* Homer starts the book as follows:

> The hero of this tale which I beg the Muse to help me tell is that of a resourceful man who roamed the world after he had sacked the holy citadel of Troy. He saw the cities of many people and he learned their ways. He suffered many hardships on the high seas in his struggles to preserve his life and bring his comrades home....This is the tale I pray the divine Muse to unfold to us. Begin it, goddess, at whatever point you will.

The Myth

Odysseus goes to Troy, spends ten years there, fighting in the Trojan War, and returns on a voyage that takes another ten years, and is full of hazards and dangers. Homer's book, *The Odyssey,* can be looked upon as a travel book, about someone who "roamed the wide world." The image shown above is from a mosaic about Odysseus and the Sirens in the Bardo Museum in Tunisia.

Psychoanalytic Manifestation of the Myth

Wanderlust is the need some people have to travel, endlessly, searching, some theorists suggest, for an idealized father or mother figure. In Leland Hinsie and Robert Jean Campbell's *Psychiatric Dictionary,* 4th edition, we read (1970:807):

> ***Wanderlust.*** Morbid impulse to roam or wander, believed to be associated with the Oedipus situation in the sense that the wanderer is incessantly striving to establish affiliation with one or both parents as he experienced it, or longed to experience it, when he was a young child.

We will see, at the conclusion of *The Odyssey,* how the search for an ideal mother has played an important role in the book.

Historical Events and the Myth

A Frenchman, Alexis de Tocqueville, travels to America and later writes a book about American culture and politics, *Democracy in America.* Countless other examples of books by travelers could be offered here.

Elite Culture Manifestations of the Myth

Thomas Mann's "Death in Venice," Jonathan Swift's *Gulliver's Travels,* and many others. Some critics have argued that all novels are, in essence, about travel.

Popular Culture Manifestations of the Myth

Travel magazines, television travel shows, travel guidebooks, books by writers about their travels, sites on the Internet about tourism, purchasing cruises, tours, and visiting any city or country or combination of cities and countries. Some travelers write elaborate descriptions of their cruises or visits to various cities on sites on the Internet.

Everyday Life Manifestations of the Myth

A person takes a cruise in the Mediterranean Sea.

What this little exercise in mythic analysis suggests is that there may be mythological foundations that become removed from their sacred origins behind many of the things we do—one of which involves travel. That is, many of our activities are what Eliade has described above as "camouflaged" myths and rituals and one of those camouflaged myths and rituals involves travel. Note, also, that there were dangers that Odysseus faced in his travels—dangers that heightened the significance of his voyage just as interruptions, disruptions, and a certain element of anxiety about one's safety heighten the experience of travel for many contemporary tourists. Tourists are often swindled by taxi cab drivers, shop owners, and others in the course of their travels and sometimes face serious dangers from robbers.

Travel is associated with attributes like an adventurous personality, independence, and curiosity. Travelers frequently must deal with delays of one sort or another, must make changes in their plans, and sometimes they may even face danger—all of which heighten their feelings of adequacy and of being alive. There is generally an element of physical discomfort and sometimes even "pain" connected with international travel; travelers become exhausted from long flights necessary to travel great distances. Travel is hard work, as every traveler knows--even if you are on a cruise ship and don't have to worry about finding a place to stay and a good restaurant.

Many people consider themselves "travelers" and not "tourists," perhaps because the connotations of "tourist" are not positive. Travel, they believe, suggests effort and adventure while tourism suggests ease and passivity. But what about adventure tours, which can be quite strenuous? Even many ordinary tours, because of their rapid pace and the sightseeing involved, are also fairly strenuous. So is there a difference between being a traveler and a tourist? Not as I use the terms.

What is a Tourist?

There is no universally accepted definition of tourism; different scholars define it in different ways. The World Tourism Organization defines tourism as follows:

> It comprises the activities of persons traveling to and staying in places outside their usual environment for not more than one consecutive year for leisure, business, and other purposes not related to the exercise of an activity remunerated from within the place visited.
>
> http://www.world-tourism.org/statistics/tsa_project/TSA20depth/chapters/ch3-1.htm

For many people, the term tourism has negative connotations, because of the supposed superficiality and regimentation of some package tours and because of the connection of tourism with consumer culture.

The Tourist as Model for Modern Man and Woman

In his classic book, *The Tourist: A New Theory of the Leisure Class,* Dean MacCannell defines the tourist as the model for modern man and woman (1976:1):

> Tourist" is used to mean two things in this book. It designates actual tourists: sightseers, mainly middle-class, who are at this moment deployed through the entire world in search of experience. I want the book to serve as a sociological study of this group. But I should make it known that, from the beginning, I intended something more. The tourist is an actual person, or real people are actually tourists. At the same time, "the tourist" is one of the best models for modern-man-in-general. I am equally interested in "the tourist" in this second, metasociological sense of the term. Our first apprehension of modern civilization, it seems to me, emerges in the mind of the tourist.

For MacCannell, then, tourists are mainly middle-class sightseers in quest of experience, who also serve as models or prototypes for modern man. This would suggest, if you push this notion to its logical conclusion, that to be a human, or, at least, a modern man (and woman) is to be a tourist. Homo sapiens (man and woman, the thinker) has been replaced by homo tornos (man and woman, the traveler and tourist).

Seafarers and the Self

The cruise industry is an important part of tourism and many people only take cruises. It is an excellent way for people who are elderly or who have problems with walking. On cruises, you see many people in wheelchairs or walking with a cane. Before the Covid-19 pandemic, the cruise industry was flourishing and cruise lines were building cruise ships as fast as they could. The cruise industry survived the pandemic and will be using all of the ships they have built, and are building.

Forbes offers some statistics on the cruise industry:

> According to the Cruise Lines International Association (CLIA), the world's largest cruise industry trade organization, 32 million passengers are set to travel on cruise ships in 2020, up from 30 million in 2019. Since 2009, cruise ship passengers have grown from 17.8 million to 30 million, an annual growth rate of 5.4%.
>
> More significantly, cruise industry revenues have grown even faster, from approximately 15.7 billion in 2010 to an estimated 31.5 billion in 2020, a compounded rate of growth of 7.2%. Worldwide, the cruise industry generated $150 billion in direct and indirect revenues. The

> industry provided 1.177 million jobs and an annual payroll of $50.24 billion, an average salary of around $45,000. Contrary to the widely held belief that cruise industry jobs are low-paying, the industry has among the highest average salaries in the tourism and recreation sector.
>
> There are currently 278 ocean cruise line ships operating across 55 cruise companies with another 19 ships scheduled to debut in 2020. Passenger carrying capacity is scheduled to increase by one-third between 2020 and 2025. In addition, there are now over 500 river cruise ships.
>
> https://www.forbes.com/sites/joemicallef/2020/01/20/state-of-the-cruise-industry-smooth-sailing-into-the-2020s

We can see, then, that cruising is a popular form of tourism and cruising offers people an identity that I describe as the "Seafaring Self." My wife and I have taken around a dozen cruises over the past thirty years, but on our cruises, we've met people who seem addicted to cruising and who have taken sixty and eighty cruises. There may be an element of addiction to cruising. Whatever the case, taking cruises and visiting exotic destinations provides many people with an important kind of identity—a "world traveler."

Odysseus as the Ur Seafarer

At the end of the book, in his chapter "Odysseus and Penelope," Homer offers the paradigmatic travel report:

> He began with his first victory over the Cicones and his visit to the fertile land where the Lotus-eaters live. He spoke of what the Cyclops did, and the price he had him pay for the gallant men he ruthlessly devoured. He told her of his stay with Aeolus, so friendly when he came and helpful when he left; and how the gale, since Providence would not let him reach his home so soon, had caught him up once more and driven him in misery down the highways of the fish. Next came his call at Teleplus on the Laestrygonian coast, where the savages destroyed his fleet and all his fighting men, the black ship that carried him being the only one to get away. He spoke of Circe and her magic arts; of how he sailed across the mouldering Halls of Hades to consult the soul of the Theban Tiresias and saw all his former comrades and the mother who had born him and nursed him as a child.

Whatever the case, whether one is a traveler or a tourist (or both), whether one takes a cruise on a small river ship or a gigantic ocean cruise ship with 6,000 other passengers, many people who visit other cities and other countries are likely motivated, at the unconscious level, by the myth of Odysseus and all books by travel writers and all travel articles and books are, in the final analysis, variations of the UR travel book and story, *The Odyssey.* Travel is beneficial to people in many ways, and one thing it does is to confer on people who visit other lands a positive identity: a world traveler.

Chapter 19

Coda

How I Wrote This Book:

An Exercise in Autobiographical Identity

I like to explain to my readers how I write my books. Some writers plan every chapter out before doing any writing and their books involve, to a considerable extent, filling in and enhancing their outlines. But I take a different approach. Once I get an idea for a book, I do a lot of brainstorming about the topic of the book, but I have no idea how it will end up when I start—except in very general terms.

One day, when I was writing in my journal, the idea of doing something on identity suddenly popped into my head. It might be because I had suggested that my wife read *Cards of Identity,* one of my favorite comic novels. Here is the start of my book in my journal when I wrote "I may start a new project on identity."

Figure 19.1: Author's Journal Note. Speculation on Starting a Book on Identity.

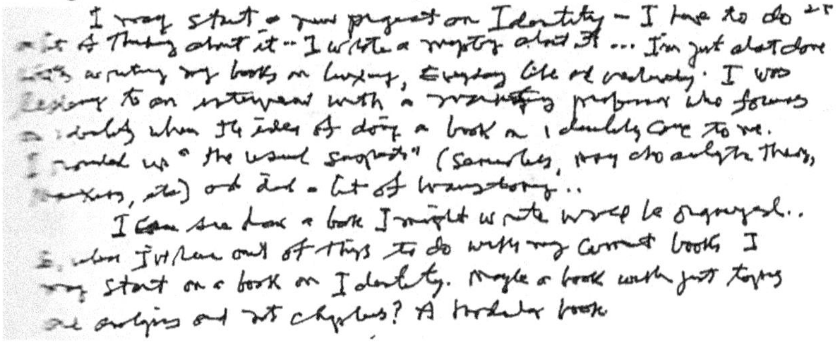

Whatever the reason, I started writing down ideas in my journal. I showed a copy of my first jottings at the beginning of this book. I was at the beginning of journal number 104 and continued brainstorming in that journal on many pages. I began writing journals in 1954, which explains why I have so many journals. It is my practice to divide some journal pages into four columns for my brainstorming and I offer an example of one of these pages below.

Since I am a semiotician, I started the book as an essay on the semiotics of identity, not knowing where I would go after I wrote the essay. Then I decided that I would offer chapters on a psychoanalytic perspective on identity, a

Marxist view of identity, and a sociological view of the subject. This design goes back to the seventies when I wrote a book, *Media Analysis Techniques,* that has chapters on semiotic theory, psychoanalytic theory, sociological theory, and Marxist theory in the first part of the book and then chapters in which I apply these theories to various topics such as news, football, *Murder on the Orient Express,* video games, and cell phones.

Figure 19.2: Author's Journal Note: Brainstorming Page.

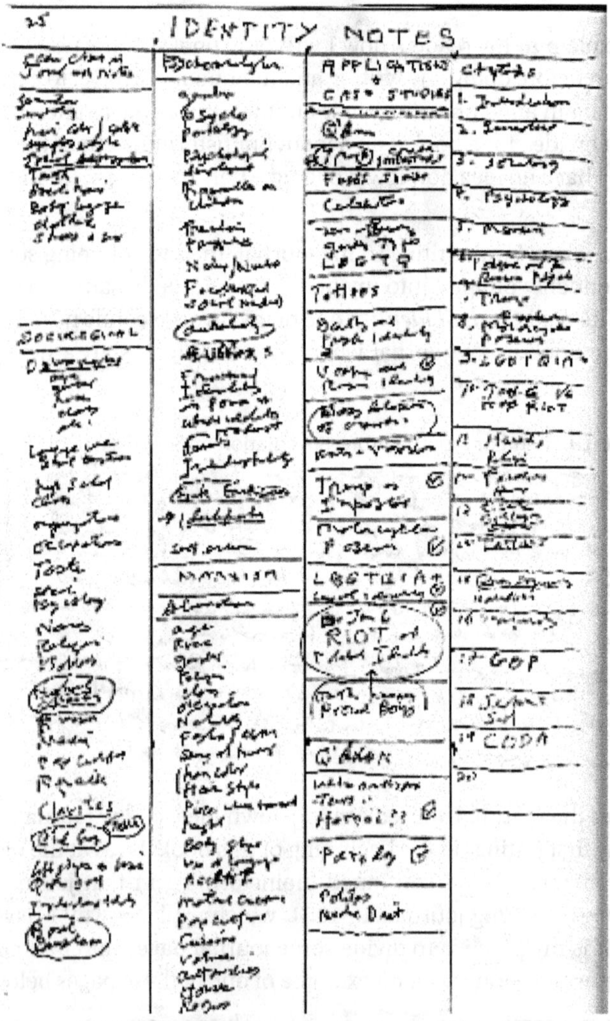

I had decided to use the same structure as I used in *Media Analysis Techniques* and many other books in which I devote the first part of the book to theories and the second part of the book to applications. But I had no idea of what topics

I would discuss in the applications part of the book and it was a struggle for me to find topics that would deal with interesting aspects of identity.

Figure 19.3: Identity Chart From Author's Journal.

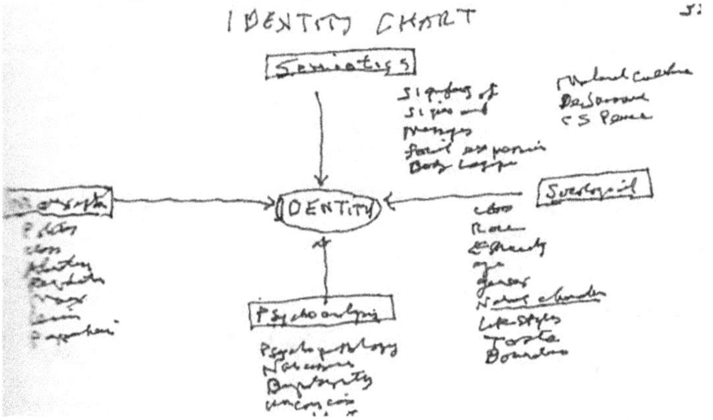

In my journal, I had made a list of areas to consider in writing the book in a four columned chart dealing with age, gender, religion, class, occupation, education, tattoos, and the 1/6 insurrection at the Capitol, but I didn't know how to translate my interest in a given topic into a chapter. These chapters would be relatively short and would use many quotations from writers to help me make my arguments.

That was the difficult part of writing the book, but I found that once I started a chapter, I was able to write it without too much trouble. I tend to write quickly and then spend time revising and rewriting my first and second drafts. When I write, I like to cite sources who have important things to say about a given topic, so you will see many quotations in my books—from philosophers, professors, scholars, journalists, and writers of all kinds.

I also like to ask people with expertise in certain areas to contribute short boxed inserts for the book and you read several inserts when you read the book. In this book, you will read inserts by a psychoanalyst, a semiotician, a Marxist, and a sociologist. Their inserts will provide different perspectives on the subject of identity. On some topics, I devoted part of the page to thinking up different aspects of the topic that I might discuss.

In essence, what I did on these pages is outline ideas for the chapters, though I didn't always use all of the topics I listed. I have other pages in my journal devoted to each topic, though some outlines are not as elaborate as the January 6 insurrection one. Identity is a subject of considerable interest. I checked on identity on Google in March 2021 and got 812 million results. I got 1,680 million results for self-concept and 1,600 million for self-identity. I checked on the

Amazon.com book section and found 40,000 books for "identity" (all aspects of) and 200,000 books for "self" and 80,000 books for "self-love."

Figure 19.4: Brainstorming on the January 6 Insurrection at the Capitol in Author's Journal.

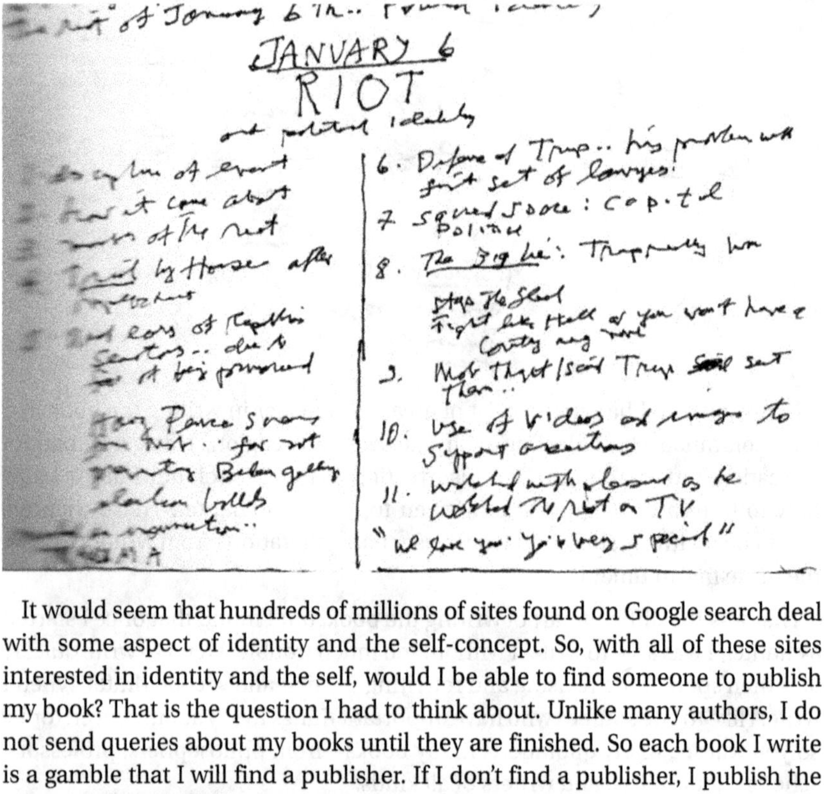

It would seem that hundreds of millions of sites found on Google search deal with some aspect of identity and the self-concept. So, with all of these sites interested in identity and the self, would I be able to find someone to publish my book? That is the question I had to think about. Unlike many authors, I do not send queries about my books until they are finished. So each book I write is a gamble that I will find a publisher. If I don't find a publisher, I publish the book on my own under the name of my press, Marin Arts.

When authors write a book, unless it is under contract, they send queries to publishers who might be interested in the book. Below I show the query I designed to send to publishers. If the publishers are interested, they request the author to send a proposal which usually involves a chapter from the book, information about its target market, how it is different from other books on the subject, a vita, and various other questions. A typical proposal might end up being thirty or forty pages long. This proposal is usually sent to some experts (typically professors for academic books) for an evaluation but in some cases, the entire manuscript is sent off.

If the evaluations are positive, there is a good chance the book will be published, and if they are very negative, it is unlikely that the publisher will accept the book. If they are split, the editor might send the book to another professor for another evaluation. This process can take months so authors have to wait and hope for the best while the process moves on.

Below is the query I sent to publishers about the book.

Figure 19.5: Searching for Self Book Advertisement.

Arthur Asa Berger
Email: arthurasaberger@gmail.com

Searching for a Self
Perspectives on Identity

35,000 words. Many illustrations and photos by the author.
A secondary text for courses in cultural studies, sociology, psychology, etc.

Contents:
Theoretical Approaches to Identity
Introduction
Semiotic Theory and Identity
Sociological Theory and Identity
Psychoanalytic Theory and Identity
Marxism and Identity
Applications
Introduction
Vodka and Russian Identity
Trump and the Impostor Syndrome
Fashion and Identity
LGBTQIA+ and Gender Identity
and more to come.

Arthur Asa Berger is Professor Emeritus of Broadcast and Electronic Communication Arts at San Francisco State University. He has published more than 100 articles and 80 books on semiotics, media analysis, communication, humor, and tourism. His books have been translated into ten languages. He had a Fulbright to Italy in 1963 and has been a Fulbright Senior Specialist in Belarus, Argentina, and Germany.

Plus boxed inserts by a psychoanalyst, semiotician, sociologist, Marxist, and maybe others.

I have been writing and publishing books for more than fifty years. Three of the publishers who used to take my books were purchased by a gigantic English company, Taylor & Francis, so I've had to search for a "loving" editor and they are hard to find. It is one thing to write a book, but marketing that book, finding a publisher, is always a problem. Writers can take solace in knowing that countless editors have passed on trade books that have sold millions of copies and academic books that have won all kinds of prizes.

As I think about my career, I've actually written about American identity in many of my books, though I didn't think of them that way—the focus was on American pop culture, culture, everyday life, but the subtext of all of those books was on identity. So writing this book has been the culmination of a long process of writing about identity.

If you have learned something about identity as it manifests itself in countless ways, and come away from this book with new insights about identity, I will feel that writing the book has been worthwhile. Now that I've finished this book, like all writers, and my identity is that of being a writer, I'm thinking about what the next book will be about. That's what it means to be a writer.

Arthur Asa Berger
Mill Valley, California

Glossary

1/6. (January 6, 2021). The date when a mob of people, urged to do so by Donald Trump, invaded the Capitol, searching for people to kill, and trashed the building.

Aberrant Decoding. The notion, elaborated by the Italian semiotician Umberto Eco, that audiences decode or interpret texts such as television commercials and print advertisements in ways that differ from the ways the creators of these texts expect them to be decoded. Aberrant decoding is the rule rather than the exception when it comes to the mass media, according to Eco. It has been estimated that about 25 percent of advertisements and commercials are decoded aberrantly, that is, not the way the creators of the texts expected them to be decoded.

Advertisement. The word advert means "to call attention to something," and thus an advertisement is, for our purposes, a kind of text—carried by electronic or print media—that attracts attention to, stimulates a desire for, and in some cases leads to the purchase of a product or service. The convention is that commercial messages in print are called advertisements and those in electronic media are called commercials.

Alienation. In Marxist theory, capitalist societies can create enormous amounts of consumer goods, but they also inevitably generate alienation and feelings of estrangement from oneself and others in society. Alienation is functional for those who own the means of production and distribution since alienation leads to consumer cultures—ones characterized by endless and frantic consumption, which people use as an escape from their feelings of alienation. In capitalist societies, therefore, advertising plays a central role in maintaining the status quo.
See also Consumer Cultures.

Artist. We will consider an artist to be not only someone who writes, paints, sculpts, or plays musical instruments, but anyone involved in the creation or performance of a text.

Audience. Audiences are generally defined as collections of individuals who watch a television program, listen to a radio show, watch a film, spend time on social media or spend time at some kind of live artistic performance (symphony, rock band, and so on). The members of the audience may be together in one room or, in the case of television, each watching from his or her own set. In technical terms, audiences are addressees who receive mediated texts sent by an addresser. For advertisers, securing the right audiences is crucial because it doesn't pay to advertise to people who either aren't interested or can't afford the product or service being advertised. The media, in economic terms, can be held to deliver audiences to advertisers.

Borderline. George Simon describes the borderline personality as someone who has "a fractured and unstable sense of self and can exhibit a wide variety of high-risk behaviors, including extreme emotional volatility, self-injurious acts and gestures, and sometimes even breaks with reality. So helping folks with borderline personality disturbances achieve a more integrated, stable sense of self is a real challenge."

Bourdieu, Pierre. He is an influential French sociologist who argued that taste is tied to our socioeconomic status or our economic and cultural capital and is shaped more by social forces than personal preferences.

Popular. Popular is one of the most difficult terms used in discourse about the arts and the media. The term means "appealing to a large number of people." It comes from the Latin *popularis,* which means "of the people." Separating the popular and elite arts has become increasingly problematic in recent years and the idea that they are radically different has been rejected by postmodern theorists. For example, is an opera shown on television an example of elite or popular culture?

Brands. Brands create emotional ties between individuals and certain products or services who will purchase them throughout their lives. From a semiotic perspective, brands are signs people use to display their taste or wealth and to help them fashion an identity. The fact that certain companies prominently attach their logos to what they make helps users solidify their sense of style and discrimination and their identities.

Celebrity. A celebrity is someone who is well known by people for reasons that are difficult to determine. They play a role as influencers in shaping people's consumption practices.

Claritas. A market research company that claims there are sixty-six different kinds of consumers in the United States, each of which tends to be found in certain Zip codes. They argue that "birds of a feather flock together" and give each of the groupings jazzy names such as "Blue Blood Estates" and "Shotguns and Pickups." People who purchase luxury goods tend to live in areas full of luxury homes.

Class. From a linguistic standpoint, a class is any group of things that have something in common. We use the term to refer to social classes, or more literally, socioeconomic classes: groups of people who share income and lifestyle. Marxist theorists argue that there is a ruling class, which shapes the ideas of the proletariat, the working classes. Advertisers are interested in socioeconomic classes and lifestyles because these phenomena are held to be the key to selling products and services.

Codes. Codes are systems of symbols, letters, words, sounds, whatever, that generate meaning. Language, for example, is a code. It uses combinations of letters that we call words to mean certain things. The relation between the word and the thing the word stands for is arbitrary, based on convention. In some cases, the term code is used to describe hidden meanings and disguised communications. Semioticians explain that people have to know certain codes if they are to interpret signs correctly.

Collective Representations. The French sociologist Emile Durkheim used this concept to deal with the fact that people are both individuals pursuing their own aims, and social animals guided by the groups and societies in which they find themselves. Collective representations are, broadly speaking, texts that reflect the beliefs and ideals of collectivities. Advertisements are designed, one could say, as collective representations that will appeal to people and help advertisers shape people's behavior. Advertisements for luxury goods have a different look and style to them from advertisements for inexpensive goods.

Communication. There are many different ways of understanding and using this term. For our purposes, communication is a process that involves the transmission of messages from senders to receivers. We often make a distinction between communication using language, verbal communication, and communication using facial expressions, body language, and other means, or nonverbal communication. In advertisements and television commercials, both verbal and nonverbal communication play very important roles.

Consumer Cultures. Consumer cultures are characterized by widespread personal consumption rather than socially conscious and useful investment in the public sphere. The focus is on private expenditure and leisure pursuits, and this leads to privatism, self-centeredness, and a reluctance to allocate resources for the public realm. Advertising is held by many critics to be a primary instrument of those who own the means of production in generating consumer lust and consumer cultures and distracting people from social and public matters. Social scientists Aaron Wildavsky and Mary Douglas suggest that there are four political cultures, which also function as consumer cultures: hierarchical or elitist, individualist, egalitarian, and fatalist. Luxury goods make up about ten percent of purchases in consumer cultures.

Culture. There are hundreds of definitions of culture. Generally speaking, from the anthropological perspective, it involves the transmission from generation to generation of specific ideas, arts, customary beliefs, ways of living, behavior patterns, institutions, and values. When applied to the arts, it generally is used to specify "elite" kinds of artworks, such as operas, poetry, classical music, and serious art.

Culture Code. A book by Clotaire Rapaille that describes consumption practices in different countries. It argues that children, up to the age of seven, become imprinted by a particular country's codes of behavior and those codes shape people's behavior for the rest of their lives. I argue in many of my writings that what we think of as a culture can be understood to be a collection of codes of behavior and thinking that people learn growing up in a culture or subculture. If you understand people's codes, you can better understand their behavior.

Cultural Studies aka Cultural Criticism. The term cultural criticism refers to the analysis of texts and various aspects of everyday life by scholars in various disciplines who use concepts from their fields of expertise to interpret mass-mediated texts, the role of the mass media, and related concerns. The focus is on what impact these texts and the media that carry them have on individuals, society, and culture. Cultural criticism involves the use of literary theory, media analysis, philosophical thought, communication theory, and various interpretive methodologies.

Defense Mechanisms. According to Freudian psychoanalytic theory, Defense Mechanisms are methods used by the ego to defend itself against pressures from the id or impulsive elements in the psyche and superego, such as conscience and guilt. Some of the more common defense mechanisms are repression (barring unconscious instinctual wishes, memories, and so on from consciousness), regression (returning to earlier stages in one's development), ambivalence (a simultaneous feeling of love and hate for a person, thing, or concept), and rationalization (offering excuses to justify one's actions). I've explained how the ego mediates between id-dominated desires to purchase products and services and superego attempts to avoid spending money.

Demographics The term demographics refers to similarities found in groups of people in terms of race, religion, gender, social class, ethnicity, occupation, place of residence, age, and so on. Demographic information plays an important role in the creation of advertising and the choice of which media to use to deliver this advertising.

Dennis, Nigel. English author who wrote the comic novel *Cards of Identity.* Wikipedia describes him as follows: In 1955, Dennis published his most notable work, *Cards of Identity, a* witty psychological satire that gained cult acclaim. The novel was converted into a play the following year. Members of the Identity

Club gather at an English country house to listen to papers discussing interesting case histories of various identity problems. The novel details many of the problems England experienced in the late forties and early fifties.

Disfunctional also Dysfunctional. In sociological thought, something is disfunctional if it contributes to the breakdown or destabilization of the entity in which it is found.

Egalitarians. They stress that everyone is equal in terms of certain needs, such as food, shelter, and access to health care. Egalitarians function as critics of the two dominant political/consumer cultures—elitist and individualist.

Ego. In Sigmund Freud's theory of the psyche, the ego functions as the executant of the id and as a mediator between the id and the superego (conscience). The ego is involved in the perception of reality and adaptation to reality. One aspect of the ego, I argue, is in helping the superego to restrain compulsive spending, which the id wishes to do.

Enclavists. Mary Douglas' term for Egalitarians.

False Consciousness. In Marxist thought, false consciousness refers to mistaken ideas that people have about their class, status, and economic possibilities. These ideas help maintain the status quo and are of great use to members of the ruling class, who wants to avoid changes in the social and economic structure of a society. Karl Marx argued that the ideas of the ruling class are always the ruling ideas in society. Marxists would argue that the belief many Americans have that they can succeed if they have enough willpower and are "elites" because they can consume at a relatively high level is an example of false consciousness.

Fatalists. They are at the bottom rungs of society—they have little political or consumer power and can only escape their status as a result of luck or chance, such as winning a lottery.

Feminist Theory. Feminist theory focuses on the roles given to women and the way they are portrayed in texts of all kinds, including one of the worst offenders—advertising. Feminist critics argue that women are typically used as sexual objects and are portrayed stereotypically in advertisements and other kinds of texts, and this has negative effects on both men and women.

Freud, Sigmund. Wikipedia describes him as follows: (/frɔɪd/ *FROYD*;[3] German: [ˈziːk.mʊnt ˈfʁɔʏt]; born **Sigismund Schlomo Freud**; 6 May 1856 – 23 September 1939) was an Austrian neurologist and the founder of psychoanalysis, a clinical method for treating psychopathology through dialogue between a patient and a psychoanalyst.

Functional. In sociological thought, the term functional refers to the contribution an institution makes to the maintenance of society or an institution or entity. Something functional helps maintain the system in which it is found. Many social scientists are functionalists.

Functional Alternative. This term refers to something that takes the place of something else. For example, professional football can be seen as a functional alternative to religion. I argue in this book that a department store can be seen as a modern functional alternative to medieval cathedrals.

Gender. Gender is the sexual category of an individual: male or female, and the behavioral traits that are connected with each category. Gender is now held to be "socially constructed," which means it is our societies that determine what we think about gender. The binary distinction between males and females is no longer considered valid and individuals now have a range of possibilities when defining their gender.

GOP. The GOP stands for the Grand Old Party, which is one of the ways that the Republican Party has been described. In recent years the nature of the Republican Party has changed and the people Republicans vote into power tend to be ideological extremists.

Grid-Group Theory. This theory is based on the work of social anthropologist Mary Douglas, who argued that there are four (and only four) consumer cultures or lifestyles in modern societies, based on the degree to which the groups have weak or strong boundaries and whether members have few or many rules and prescriptions to follow. The four lifestyles are in competition with one another and are antagonistic but need each other.

Haredi. This term refers to strictly Orthodox or as they are commonly described as ultra-Orthodox Jews. The males can be recognized by the clothes they wear—wide-brimmed black hats and black suits and the women by long skirts and head coverings. Haredi have ultimate reverence for the Torah and tend to limit their contact with the outside world.

Hierarchical Elitists. These people are one of the four lifestyles in Grid-Group theory and are at the top of the economic and power pyramid. They believe that hierarchy is needed for society to run smoothly. They have a sense of obligation to those beneath them. Elitists and individualists make up the core of luxury purchasers since they have the social and economic capital needed to buy luxury products and services.

Hypothesis. A hypothesis is essentially a guess about something. Social scientists use the term to suggest that they have ideas that may be interesting and even correct, but which they have not been able to verify.

Id. The Id in Freud's theory of the psyche (technically known as his structural hypothesis) is that element of the psyche that is the representative of a person's drives. In *New Introductory Lectures on Psychoanalysis,* Freud called it "a chaos, a cauldron of seething excitement." It also is the source of energy, but lacking direction, it needs the ego to harness it and control it. In popular thought, it is connected to impulse, lust, and "I want it all now" behavior. Many advertisements, for all kinds of products and services, appeal to Id elements in our psyches.

Identity. Our identities are affected by our birth order, by our hair color, by how tall or short we are, by our intelligence, by our occupation, by race, by our religion, by our nationality, by the socio-economic level of our parents (or being raised in a single-parent family), by where we are born and where we grow up, by the language we learn, by the way we use language, by our fashion tastes, by our gender, by our education, by our psychological makeup, by chance experiences we have, by the people we marry (if we marry) and by countless other factors. As Nigel Dennis writes in his *Cards of Identity,* "Identity is the answer to everything. There is nothing that cannot be seen in terms of identity. We are not going to pretend that there is the slightest argument about *that.*" My book is an attempt to help us better understand identity and the role it plays in our politics, attitudes towards race, occupations, religions, subcultures, popular culture, psyches, and just about everything else one can think of.

Ideology. An ideology is a logically coherent, integrated explanation of social, economic, and political matters that helps establish the goals and direct the actions of a group or political entity. People act (and vote or don't vote) based on an ideology they hold, even though they may not have articulated it or thought about it.

Image. Defining images is extremely difficult. In my book *Seeing Is Believing: An Introduction to Visual Communication,* I define an image as "a collection of signs and symbols—what we find when we look at a photograph, a film still, a shot of a television screen, a print advertisement, or just about anything." The term is used for mental as well as physical representations of things. Images often have powerful emotional effects on people and historical significance.

Impostor. An impostor is someone who pretends to have an identity. Impostors are different from impersonators, who pretend to be someone in particular.

Imprints. According to the French psychoanalyst and marketing theorist Clotaire Rapaille, children in all countries are imprinted, by the age of seven, by the culture of the country in which they grow up. These imprints then shape, to a considerable degree, their thinking and behavior when they are adults. He discusses this in his book *Culture Codes.*

Individualists. In Grid-Group theory, individualists are members of a lifestyle that believes that the basic function of government is to prevent crime and invasion by foreign powers. They are competitive and stress the importance of individual initiative.

Intertextuality. This theory argues that texts (works of art) of all kinds are influenced to varying degrees by texts that preceded them. Sometimes, as in the case of parody, the relationship is overt, but in many cases, creators of texts are influenced by stylistic practices or thematic ones from earlier works. We can say, then, that intertextuality involves making allusions to, imitating, modifying, or adapting previously created texts and styles of expression.

Isolates. The term Mary Douglas uses for the lifestyle described by others as Fatalists.

Ivy League. This is the name for some elite universities such as Harvard, Yale, Columbia, Dartmouth, and Cornell that are located on the East Coast in America and are very selective.

Latent Functions. Latent functions are hidden, unrecognized, and unintended results of some activity, entity, or institution. They are contrasted by social scientists with manifest functions, which are recognized and intended. The manifest function of buying a luxury automobile may be because it is technically superior to other cars but the latent function of buying the car is to show that one can afford it and to gain status.

LGBTQIA+. The letters above stand for Lesbian, Gay, Bisexual, Transgender, Queer/Questioning, Intersexual, Asexual/Aromantic, and other identities in Queerness—all of which are possibilities in non-binary gender identities

Lifestyle. Literally style of life, lifestyle refers to the way people live—to the decisions they make about how to decorate their homes (and where the homes are located), the cars they drive, the clothes they wear, the foods they eat, the restaurants they visit, and where they go for vacations. Lifestyles tend to be coherent or logically connected, and they play an important part in market research because lifestyles tend to shape consumption patterns in individuals.

Manifest Functions. The manifest functions of an activity, entity, or institution are those that are obvious and intended. Manifest functions contrast with latent functions, which are hidden and unintended. The manifest function of advertising is to sell products and services; the latent function is to sell the political order. See also Latent Functions.

Marx, Karl. He was a German economist, political theorist, journalist, and socialist revolutionary, whose ideas had an enormous impact in many areas.

Some media scholars use Marxist ideas to expose the hidden ideologies located in popular culture texts and various aspects of everyday life.

Mass Communication. This term refers to the transfer of messages, information, and texts from a sender to receivers, in many cases a large number of people, a mass audience. This transfer is done through the technologies of the mass media—newspapers, magazines, television programs, films, records, computers, the Internet, and CD-ROMs. A sender is often a person in a large media organization, the messages are public, and the audience tends to be large and varied. With the development of social media such as Facebook and Instagram, now many people can communicate with large numbers of people.

Medium (plural: Media). A medium is a means of delivering messages, information, or texts to audiences. There are different ways of classifying the media. One of the most common ways is as follows: print (newspapers, magazines, books, billboards), electronic (radio, television, computers, CD-ROMs, the Internet), and photographic (photographs, films, videos). Various critics have suggested that the main function of the commercial media is to deliver audiences to advertisers and that everything else the media does is of secondary importance.

Metaphor. A metaphor is a figure of speech that conveys meaning by analogy. For example, "My love is a rose." It is important to realize that metaphors are not confined to poetry and literary works but, according to some linguists, are the fundamental way in which we make sense of things and find meaning in the world. A simile is a weaker form of metaphor that uses either "like" or "as" in making an analogy. Metaphors are an important element in advertising. For example, Fidji perfume had a campaign that was explicitly metaphoric: Woman is an island. If the advertisement had said "Woman is like an island," that would have been a simile. According to linguists, metonymy is a figure of speech that conveys information by association and is, along with metaphor, one of the most important ways people convey information to one another. We tend not to be aware of our use of metonymy, but whenever we use association to get an idea about something (Rolls-Royce signifies wealth) we are thinking metonymically. A form of metonymy that involves seeing a whole in terms of a part or vice versa is called synecdoche. Using the Pentagon to stand for the American military is an example of synecdoche.

Modernism. The period before postmodernism, from roughly 1900 to 1960, when postmodernism became culturally dominant. Modernism's esthetics and values, its belief in master narratives (like its belief in progress), and grand theories were rejected by postmodernist thinkers and people affected by postmodernist thought.

Myth. Myths are conventionally understood to be sacred stories about gods and cultural heroes (and in more recent years, mass-mediated heroes and heroines) who are used to transmit a culture's basic belief system to younger generations and to explain natural and supernatural phenomena. This book argues that myths play an important role in shaping our behavior in many areas of life, which I describe in what I call the "myth model."

Myth Model. This model argues that myths inform many aspects of our lives, though we may not recognize this is the case. It shows how myths can be found in psychoanalytic theory, historical experience, elite culture, popular culture, and everyday life.

National character. This theory argues that people who grow up in a country can be characterized by certain values, beliefs, and distinctive behaviors. Thus, there is a big difference between people in different countries—a topic explored by Clotaire Rapaille in his book *The Culture Code.* People growing up in the same country, in different regions, also differ in many ways.

Nonfunctional. In sociological thought, something is nonfunctional if it is neither functional nor dysfunctional, but plays no role in the entity in which it is found.

Nonverbal Communication. Our body language, facial expressions, styles of dress, and hairstyles are examples of our communicating feelings and attitudes (and a sense of who we are) without words. In our everyday lives, a great deal of our communication is done nonverbally.

Peirce, C.S. He is one of the founding fathers of the study of signs and gave the science its name, semiotics, a term based on the Greek word for sign, sēmeîon. He was a professor at Harvard and produced many works on semiotic theory. Peirce is considered to be one of America's foremost philosophers.

Phallic Symbol. In Freudian theory, an object that resembles the penis either by shape or function is described as a phallic symbol. Symbolism is a defense mechanism of the ego that permits hidden or repressed sexual or aggressive thoughts to be expressed in a disguised form. For a discussion of this topic see Freud's book *An Interpretation of Dreams.* I offer the example of the Washington Monument as a gigantic phallic symbol, named after the father of our country. The term phallocentric is used to suggest societies that are dominated by males, and the ultimate source of this domination, which shapes our institutions and cultures, is the male phallus. In this theory, a link is made between male sexuality and male power.

Popular Culture. Popular culture is a term that identifies certain kinds of texts, generally, mass-mediated, that appeal to a large number of people. But mass communication theorists often identify "popular" with "mass" and suggest that if something is popular, it must be of poor quality, appealing to the mythical "lowest common denominator." Popular culture is generally held to be the opposite of elite culture—arts that require certain levels of sophistication and refinement to be appreciated, such as ballet, opera, poetry, and classical music. Many critics now question this popular culture/elite culture polarity.

Porsche automobiles. Porsche has a cult following because its cars are both mechanically advanced and very long-lasting. Its fans would say they are stylistically beautiful, as well. Porsche is owned by Volkswagen automobiles.

Postmodernism. This theory states that a new kind of culture has developed in the United States and elsewhere, since approximately 1960, which rejected the values and beliefs of the modernist society that had been dominant until that time. One theorist of postmodernism argues that it involves "incredulity toward metanarratives," by which he means the rejection of the overarching religious, social, political, aesthetic, and moral theories of the modernist period that had shaped people's thinking and their lives. Postmodernism is associated with stylistic eclecticism and a rejection of the split between elite and popular culture. The theory is very controversial and important facets of it are explored in my books *Postmortem for a Postmodernist* (a postmodern mystery) and *The Portable Postmodernist/*

Psychoanalytic Theory. Sigmund Freud can be said to be the founding father of psychoanalytic theory. He argued that the human psyche has three levels: consciousness, preconsciousness, and the unconscious, which is the largest area of the psyche and an area not able to be accessed by individuals. What is important, psychoanalytic theorists argue, is that the unconscious shapes and affects our mental functioning and our behavior. Another of his theories posited three forces in the psyche: the id (desire), the ego (reason), and the superego (guilt), which are continually battling with one another for domination. Freud believed that sexuality and what he called "the Oedipus Complex" play a dominant role in human behavior, even if their presence is not recognized.

Psychographics In marketing, the term psychographics is used to deal with groups of people who have similar psychological characteristics or profiles. It differs from demographics, which marketers use to focus on social and economic characteristics that people have in common.

QAnon. Wikipedia describes QAnon as "a disproven and discredited far-right conspiracy theory alleging that a cabal of Satan-worshipping cannibalistic pedophiles is running a global child sex-trafficking ring and plotting against former U.S. President Donald Trump, who is fighting the cabal." The cabal, for QAnoners, is made up of Democrats.

Rapaille, Clotaire. French psychoanalyst and marketer who wrote *The Culture Code* and *The Global Code,* which deal with how different nationalities and how new global elites shape purchasing decisions.

Rationalization. In Freudian thought, a rationalization is a defense mechanism of the ego that creates an excuse to justify an action (or inaction when an action is expected). Ernest Jones, who introduced the term, used it to describe logical and rational reasons that people give to justify behavior that is really caused by unconscious and irrational determinants. We often use rationalizations to justify behavior that is not constructive.

Role Sociologists describe a role as a way of behavior that we learn in a society and that is appropriate to a particular situation. A person generally plays many roles with different people during the hours of the day, such as a parent (family), worker (job), and spouse (marriage). We also use the term to describe the parts actors have in mass-mediated texts.

Saussure, Ferdinand de. He was one of the founding fathers of the science of semiotics. His book, *Course in General Linguistics,* played a major role in the development of semiotics. He called his science "semiology,' which means, literally speaking, words about signs. He wrote that a sign is made up of two things: a signifier (word or thing) and a signified (what the signifier means; that is, a concept. The relationship between a signifier and a signified is arbitrary and based on convention, which means that the meanings of signs can change over time. There are, to simplify matters, two schools of semiotics: Saussure's and Peirce's.

Self. This term is very difficult to define and because of that, there are countless definitions of the concept. Generally, a self is held to refer to a coherent and satisfying sense of identity and a recognition of the fact that although in many respects we are like all others, we are all also different from everyone else.

Semiotics Literally, the term semiotics means "the science of signs." Sēmeîon is the Greek term for sign. A sign is anything that can be used to stand for anything else. According to C. S. Peirce, one of the founders of the science, a sign "is something which stands to somebody for something in some respect or capacity." Semiotics is one of the core disciplines used by cultural studies scholars.

Sign The basic concept in semiotics, the science of signs (from the Greek word sēmeîon, sign) that deals with how we find meaning in images and other kinds of communication. Ferdinand de Saussure, one of the founding fathers of semiotics, argued that a sign is made up of a signifier (a sound or object) and a signified (a concept). The relation between the signifier and the signified is arbitrary and not natural. C. S. Peirce, another founding father of semiotics, had a different notion. He said a sign is "something which stands to somebody for something in some respect or capacity."

Social Control. Social controls are ideas, beliefs, values, and more people get from their societies that shape their beliefs and behavior. People are both individuals with certain distinctive physical and emotional characteristics and desires and at the same time members of societies. And people are shaped to a certain degree by the institutions found in these societies.

Socialization. Socialization refers to the processes by which societies teach individuals how to behave: what rules to obey, roles to assume, and values to hold. Socialization was traditionally done by the family, educators, religious figures, and peers. The mass media in general and advertising, in particular, seem to have usurped this function to a considerable degree nowadays, with consequences that are not always positive.

Socioeconomic Class. A socioeconomic class is a categorization of people according to their incomes and related social status and lifestyles. In Marxist thought, there are ruling classes that shape the consciousness of the working classes, and history is, in essence, a record of class conflict.

Stereotypes. Stereotypes are commonly held, simplistic, and inaccurate group portraits of categories of people. Stereotypes can be positive, negative, or mixed, but generally, they are negative. Stereotyping involves making gross overgeneralizations. (All Mexicans, Chinese, Jews, African-Americans, WASPS, Americans, lawyers, doctors, professors, and so on, are held to have certain characteristics, usually negative.)

Subculture. Any complex society is made up of numerous subcultures that differ from the dominant culture in terms of such matters as ethnicity, race, religion, sexual orientation, beliefs, values, and tastes. Often members of subcultures are marginalized and victimized by members of the dominant culture.

Superego. In Freud's structural hypothesis, the superego is the agency in our psyches related to conscience and morality. The superego is involved with processes such as approval and disapproval of wishes based on their morality, critical self-observation, and a sense of guilt over wrongdoing. The functions of the superego are largely unconscious and are opposed to id elements in our psyches. Mediating between the two and trying to balance them are our egos.

Symbol. Literally speaking, a symbol is something that stands for something else. The term comes from the Greek word *symballein* which means "to put together." Advertisers use symbols because they have powerful emotional effects on people. Think, for example, of all that is found in three symbols: the cross, the Star of David, and the crescent. In C.S. Peirce's theory of semiotics, there are three kinds of signs: icons, which communicate by resemblance; indexes, which communicate by cause and effect; and symbols, whose meaning must be learned. Advertisers make use of symbols because of their power to affect human emotions.

Text. For our purposes, a text is, broadly speaking, any work of art in any medium. Critics use the term text as a convenience—so they don't have to name a given work all the time or use various synonyms. There are problems involved in deciding what the text is when we deal with serial texts, such as soap operas or comics.

Theory. I make a distinction between theories and concepts. Theories, as I use the term, are expressed in language and systematically and logically attempt to explain and predict phenomena being studied. They differ from concepts, which define phenomena that are being studied, and from models, which are abstract, usually graphic, and explicit about what is being studied. For example, Freud developed psychoanalytic theory and one of the concepts in this theory is what he called the unconscious.

Typology. We will understand a typology to be a system of classification of things that is done to clarify matters. Typologies are important because we can use them to see relationships of interest.

Uses and Gratifications. This sociological theory argues that researchers should pay attention to the way audiences use the media (or certain texts or genres of texts, such as soap operas, mysteries, police shows) and the gratifications they get from their use of these texts and the media. Uses and gratifications researchers focus, then, on how audiences use the media and not on how the media affect audiences.

Values. Values are abstract and general beliefs or judgments about what is right and wrong, and what is good and bad, that have implications for individual behavior and social, cultural, and political entities. There are some problems with values from a philosophical point of view. First, how does one determine which values are correct and good and which aren't? That is, how do we justify values? Are values objective or subjective? Second, what happens when there is a conflict between groups, each of which holds a central value that conflicts with that of another group?

Youth Culture Youth cultures are subcultures formed by young people around some area of interest, usually connected with leisure and entertainment, such as rock music, computer games, hacking, and so on. Typically, youth cultures adopt distinctive ways of dressing and develop institutions that cater to their needs. Youth cultures and young people, though they may have "anti-establishment beliefs," are particularly susceptible to lifestyle fads.

References

Allen, Woody. 1978. *Getting Even.* New York, NY: Vintage Books.

Bakhtin, Mikhail. 1984. *Rabelais and His World.* Bloomington, Indiana: Indiana University Press.

Barthes, Roland. 1972. *Mythologies.* New York, NY: Hill & Wang.

Berger, Arthur Asa. 2005. *Mistake in Identity.* Lanham, MD: Altamira Press/Rowman & Littlefield.

Berger, Arthur Asa. 2019. *Three Tropes on Trump.* New York, NY: Peter Lang.

Berger, Arthur Asa. 2020. *Media and Communication Research Methods: An Introduction to Qualitative and Quantitative Approaches.* Thousand Oaks, CA: Sage Publications.

Berger, John. 1972. *Ways of Seeing.* London: Penguin Books.

Bottomore, T.B. and M. Rubel, (Eds.) 1964. *Karl Marx, Selected Writings in Sociology and Social Philosophy.* New York, NY: McGraw-Hill.

Bourdieu, Pierre. 1993. *Sociology in Question.* Thousand Oaks, CA: Sage.

Brenner, Charles. 1974. *An Elementary Textbook of Psychoanalysis.* Garden City, NY: Doubleday.

Brunskill, David. "Social Media, Social Avatar and the Psyche: Is Facebook Good For Us?" *Australian Psychiatry 21* (6), 524-532.

Butler, Judith. 1999. *Gender Trouble: Feminism and the Subversion of Identity.* New York, NY: Routledge.

Chandler, Daniel. 2002. *Semiotics: The Basics.* London: Routledge.

Cohen, Erik. "Toward a Sociology of International Tourism," in Kotler, et al. *Marketing for Hospitality and Tourism.* 2nd Ed. 1999. Upper Saddle River, NY: Prentice-Hall.

Coleman, Lee. "What is America? A Study of Alleged American Traits." *Social Forces.* Vol. XIX, No.4, 1941.

Consumer Reports. "Most Popular Brands of Cars." Feb. 16, 2021.

Danesi, Marcel. 2017. *Concise Dictionary of Popular Culture.* Lanham, MD: Rowman & Littlefield.

Dennis, Nigel. 1955. *Cards of Identity.* New York, NY: Vanguard Press.

de Saussure, Ferdinand. 1915/1966. *Course in General Linguistics.* New York, NY: McGraw-Hill.

de Tocqueville, Alexis. 1835/1956. *Democracy in America.* New York, NY: Mentor Books.

Douglas, Mary. "In Defence of Shopping," in Falk, Pasi and Colin Campbell, (Eds). 1997. *The Shopping Experience.* London: Sage Publications.

Eco, Umberto. 1976. *A Theory of Semiotics.* Bloomington, Indiana: Indiana University Press.

Ekman, Paul (with Terrence J. Sejnowski). 1992. *Facial expression Understanding:* Report to the National Science Foundation. Arlington, VA: National Science Foundation.

Eliade, Mircea 1961. *The Sacred and the Profane.* New York, NY: Harper & Row.

Erikson, Erik. 1964. *Insight and Responsibility.* New York, NY: W.W. Norton.

Fandos, Nicholas. "Democrats Trace Trump Mob's Path in Chilling Detail." Feb. 11, 2021. *The New York Times.*

Frankel, Todd. "A Majority of the People Arrested for Capitol Insurrection had a History of Financial Trouble." *The Washington Post.* Feb. 10, 2021.

Gorer, Geoffrey and John Rickman. 1961. *The People of Great Russia: A Psychological Study.* New York: W.W. Norton.

Gottdiener, Mark. 1997. *The Theming of America: Dreams, Visions and Commercial Spaces.* Boulder, Colorado: Westview.

Hinsie, Leland R. and Robert Jean Campbell. 1970. *Psychiatric Dictionary.* 4th Ed. New York, NY: Oxford University Press.

Homer. 1946. *The Odyssey.* New York, NY: Penguin Books.

http://www.genderagenda.net/LGBTIQdefinition.htm

http://www.perseus.tufts.edu/hopper/text?doc=Perseus:abo:tlg,0086,035:1:1253a

http://www.world-tourism.org/statistics/tsa_project/TSA20depth/chapters/ch3-1.htm

https://counsellingresource.com/features/2016/12/05/borderline-personalities/

https://en.wikipedia.org/wiki/Haredi_Judaism

https://en.wikipedia.org/wiki/QAnon

https://en.wikipedia.org/wiki/Tattoo

https://richardcoyne.com/2018/03/10/pansemiotics/

https://www.allaboutvision.com/frames/men.htm

https://www.autobytel.com/car-buying-guides/features/10-most-reliable-german-cars-132423/

https://www.forbes.com/sites/joemicallef/2020/01/20/state-of-the-cruise-industry-smooth-sailing-into-the-2020s

https://www.marxists.org/archive/lenin/works/1917/staterev/ch02.htm

https://www.pca.org/news/2016-01-05/what-it-about-german-engineering

https://www.researchgate.net/publication/216530484_A_Life_Told_in_Ink_Tattoo_Narratives_and_the_Problem_of_the_Self_in_Late_Modern_Society

https://www.sol.lu.se/doc/1294600084.conference.721.pdf.0.Maran_semiotic_self.pdf/Maran_semiotic_self.pdf

https://www.usnews.com/news/politics/articles/2020-11-18/half-of-republicans-believe-president-tru

https://en.wikipedia.org/wiki/QAnonmp-won-election-poll-finds

https://www.academia.edu/323835/The_Cultural_Implications_of_Biosemiotics

https://www.washingtonpost.com/politics/2021/02/12/daily-202-trump-said-system-is-rigged-democrats-say-his-acquittal-will-prove-it/

Humphrey, Michael. 2021. "Trump's Tweets," in *The Conversation,* Feb. 3, 2021.

Kang, Milliam and Katherine Jones. "Why Do People Get Tattoos?" https://journals.sagepub.com/doi/10.1525/ctx.2007.6.1.42

Kaplan, Mordecai. M. 2010. *Judaism as a Civilization: Toward a Reconstruction of American-Jewish Life.* Philadelphia, PA: The Jewish Publication Society.

Klapp, Orrin E. 1969. *The Collective Search for Identity.* New York, NY: Holt, Rinehart, and Winston.

Knox, Olivier. Feb. 12, 2021. "The Daily 202: Trump said the system is 'rigged." Democrats say his acquittal will prove it." *The Washington Post.*

Lenin, Vladimir. *State and Revolution: The Experience of 1858-51.* https://www.marxists.org/archive/lenin/works/1917/staterev/ch02.htm.

Ludlow, Lynn. *San Francisco Chronicle.* (Date not known.)

MacCannell, Dean. 1976. *The Tourist: A New Theory of the Leisure Class.* New York, NY: Schocken Books.

Matsumoto, David, et al., (Eds.) 2013. *Nonverbal Communication: Science and Application.* Thousand Oaks, CA: Sage Publications.

Musil, Robert. 1965. *The Man Without Qualities.* New York, NY: Capricorn.

Norrick, Neil. R. "Intertextuality in Humor." *Humor,* Vol. 2 (2). Jan 1, 1989.

Oksanen, Atte and Jussi Turtainen. "A Life Told in Ink: Tattoo Narratives and the Problem of Self in Late Modern Society." *Contexts.* Winter, 2004.

Pappenheim, Fritz. 1967. *The Alienation of Modern Man.* New York, NY: Monthly Review Press.

Peirce, C.S. 1977. "Epigraph" in T. Sebeok, (Ed.) *A Perfusion of Signs.* Bloomington, Indiana: Indiana University Press.

Piddington, Ralph. 1963. *The Psychology of Laughter.* New York, NY: Gamut Press.

Pines, Maya. "How They Know What You Really Mean." *San Francisco Chronicle.* Oct. 13, 1982.

Rapaille, Clotaire. 2006. *The Culture Code: An Ingenious Way to Understand Why People Around the World Live and Buy as They Do.* New York, NY: Broadway Books.

Rossi, William A. 1976. *The Sex Life of the Foot and Shoe.* New York, NY: Saturday Review Press.

Rubinstein, Ruth. 1995. *Dress Codes: Meanings and Messages in American Culture.* Boulder, CO: Westview.

Saussure, Ferdinand, de. 1915/1966. *Course in General Linguistics.* New York, NY: McGraw-Hill.

Siegel, Alyssa. "Shoe Obsession: Women and Their Shoes." *Psychology Today.* March 7, 2013.

Smith, Hendrik. 1976. *The Russians.* New York, NY: Quadrangle.

Thompson, Michael, Richard Ellis, and Aaron Wildavsky. 1990. *Cultural Theory.* Boulder, CO: Westview.

Ulrich, Lawrence. "All Your Inner Mario Andretti Could Desire." *The Wall Street Journal.* July 2, 2020. p. B6.

Weiss, Raysh. "Haredim (Charedim) or Ultra-Orthodox Jews." https://www.myjewishlearning.com/article/haredim-charedim/

White. Donald. "Office Life: Executives Can Lose by a Hair." *San Francisco Chronicle.* Dec. 20, 1980.

Williams, Raymond. 1977. *Marxism and Literature.* Oxford, UK: Oxford University Press.

Zeitlin, I. 1967. *Marxism: a Re-Examination.* New York, NY: Van Nostrand.

About the Author

Arthur Asa Berger is Professor Emeritus of Broadcast and Electronic Communication Arts at San Francisco State University, where he taught between 1965 and 2003. He graduated in 1954 from the University of Massachusetts, where he majored in literature and philosophy.

He received an MA degree in journalism and creative writing from the University of Iowa in 1956. He was drafted shortly after graduating from Iowa and served in the U.S. Army in the Military District of Washington in Washington DC, where he was a feature writer and speechwriter in the District's Public Information Office. He also wrote about high school sports for *The Washington Post* on weekend evenings while in the army.

Berger spent a year touring Europe after he got out of the Army and then went to the University of Minnesota, where he received a Ph.D. in American Studies in 1965. He wrote his dissertation on the comic strip, *Li'l Abner.* In 1963-64, he had a Fulbright to Italy and taught at the University of Milan.

He spent a year as a visiting professor at the Annenberg School for Communication at The University of Southern California in Los Angeles in 1984 and two months in the fall of 2007 as a visiting professor at the School of Hotel and Tourism in Hong Kong Polytechnic University. He spent a month lecturing at Jinan University in Guangzhou and ten days lecturing at Tsinghua University in Beijing in spring, 2009. He spent a month in 2012 as a Fulbright Senior Specialist in Argentina, lecturing on semiotics and cultural criticism, a month in Minsk in 2014 lecturing on semiotics and popular culture, and two weeks lecturing on semiotics and media in Iran in 2015. He is the author of more than one hundred articles and more than eighty books on semiotics, media, popular culture, humor, and tourism.

Berger is married, has two children and four grandchildren, and lives in Mill Valley, California. He enjoys foreign travel and classical music. He can be reached by e-mail at arthurasaberger@gmail.com.

Index of Names

S

T

U

W

Z

Index of Topics

I

J

L

M

N

www.ingramcontent.com/pod-product-compliance
Lightning Source LLC
Chambersburg PA
CBHW050447280326
41932CB00013BA/2272